JUDITH OLNEY
on
BREAD

Also by Judith Olney

Summer Food
Comforting Food
Judith Olney's Entertainments
The Joy of Chocolate

JUDITH OLNEY
_on_
BREAD

by

Judith Olney

Photographs by Vincent Lee

Crown Publishers, Inc.   New York

Published by Crown Publishers, Inc., One Park Avenue, New York, New York 10016, and simultaneously in Canada by General Publishing Company Limited

CROWN is a trademark of Crown Publishers, Inc.
Manufactured in the United States of America

Library of Congress Cataloging in Publication Data

Olney, Judith.
    Judith Olney on bread.

    Includes index.
    1. Bread. I. Title.
TX769.044 1985 641.8′15   85-6723
ISBN 0-517-55899-8

BOOK DESIGN BY BARBARA RICHER

10 9 8 7 6 5 4 3 2 1
First Edition

For my dearest Nathan

ACKNOWLEDGMENTS

I wish to thank Alice Dorman, Betsy Walker, and Christopher McLachlan, my ABC's of cooking, for their inestimable help on this book. Thanks also to Rob Lehmann and Barbara Lovell, to Barbara Richer, Lois Van Hoy, and Don Witten, and especially to Betty Wall.

In New York, my appreciation for Susan Wood's and Richard Bauer's connections, accommodations, and concern is heartfelt.

My editor, Pamela Thomas, provided patience, good judgment, and good humor throughout this project, and I thank her for them.

CONTENTS

LIST OF COLOR PLATES

The
MYSTIQUE
of
BREAD MAKING

INTRODUCTION

There is nothing I like better than homemade bread, nothing in the whole realm of cooking that offers so much personal and sensory pleasure as a warm crackling loaf fresh from the oven. If when company comes there is the possibility of making only one complex food, I surely would make bread, for no other reason than that bread is the traditional sign of hospitality in Western culture. From Abraham's offering of bread to visiting angels in Genesis, to guests bringing presents of bread and salt to the family housewarming in Thomas Mann's novel *Buddenbrooks*, bread, that "belly-timber," as Rabelais called it, has always functioned as a comforting social mainstay, an object of religious significance, a euphemism for money, a symbol of mystic life force.

Putting aside the mystical aspects of bread making (and it is indeed a wondrous event to shape and form under one's own hands a bit of flour, some water, and a packet of yeast into a vital substance), homemade bread has therapeutic value both for the bread maker, as he or she kneads away aggressive tendencies, and for the consumer of the loaf, who is assured a wholesome, healthy, chemical-free product. To create this book, my assistants and I baked loaf after loaf during several wintry months. We ate heartily of all the breads for our lunch each day, and at the end of our baking time together, all remarked on how healthy we felt.

In this book I've included some unusual forms, because one of the great joys of bread making is playing with malleable dough to shape it into a variety of handsome edible objects. I have also added recipes for leftover bread and recipes for nonedible decorative breads, for bread seems to inspire thoughtful frugal cooks and artistic cooks as well. I hope you receive altogether as much pleasure baking from this book as did those of us who participated in its creation.

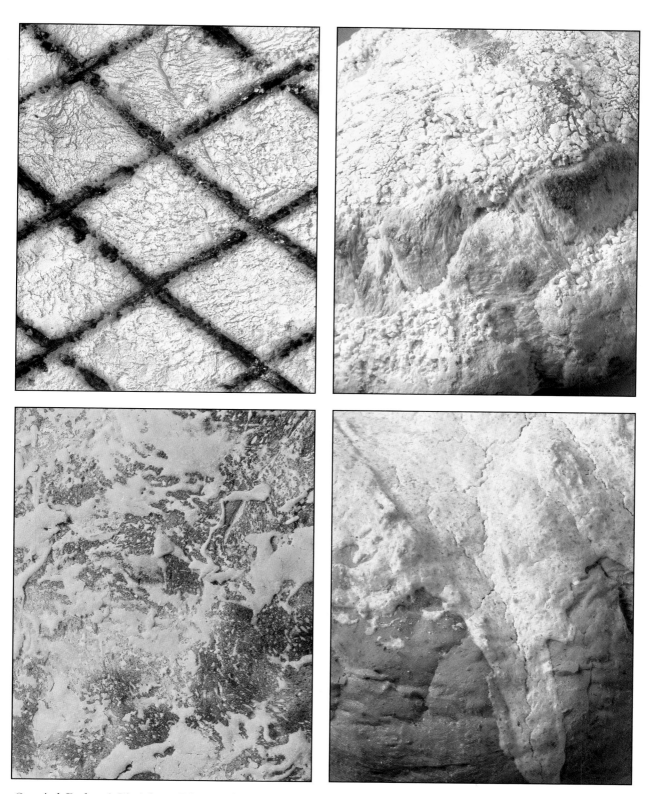

Special Bakers' Finishes: **Plate 1** *(top left). A Basket Bread with a Scorched Design;* **Plate 2** *(top right). A close-up of a Basket Bread with rough, coarse crevices;* **Plate 3** *(bottom left). The Jackson Pollock Splatter Finish;* **Plate 4** *(bottom right). A light topping for a dark loaf.*

Plate 5. The Bunch of Grapes. A huge bread, marvelous for parties. **Plate 6.** The Sourdough Bread.

ON FLOUR

Simple honest bread is composed of four ingredients—flour, water, yeast, and salt. In attempts to duplicate French bread, I have hauled back bread flour from France, used Evian water and sea salt and fresh bakers' yeast to leaven and season, and in the end decided that there was no difference discernible from this attempted purity. Plain, uniodized salt and tap water do just as well. Fresh yeast is fine when you can get it, but not necessary. French bread flour matters not one whit, particularly as it is mostly made from Canadian and American wheat anyway.

We do well to concern ourselves with flour when we bake, however, for therein lies the nutritive value of the endeavor. Further, the condition, age, and gluten strength of the flour affect the end product. There are several strengths of flour commercially available to most consumers:

1. Cake flour (soft wheat flour) is low in protein (gluten) content and, in consequence, high in starch. It is good for making biscuits. It is usually milled to a finer size than other flours, and therefore it has a greater ability to absorb moisture. It is made from "soft" wheat—particular strains that are higher in starch and that are grown in warmer climates. It has a protein content of around 8 percent.

2. All-purpose flour is of medium protein strength (around 10 to 11 percent). It can be made wholly from certain strains of wheat or it can be formulated from soft and hard wheat flours in combination.

This flour is particularly good for breads that will be aerated with baking powder. The flour is strong enough to hold its own against the pressures of expanding gases, yet sufficiently weak so that the crumb of the bread will remain tender.

3. Unbleached flour and bread flour (hard wheat flours) usually contain 12 to 15 percent protein. They are made from strains of wheat that contain more gluten and less starch, and these strains tend to be grown and "hardened off" in cold climates. This flour is ideal for plain white bread and rolls because it allows dough to hold its shape well. It is also used for puff pastry. Bread flour is bromated—that is, it has chemicals added that increase the leavening power of yeast and effect certain changes in the texture of the crumb. I prefer to use plain unbleached flour for my bread baking.

4. Self-rising flour is all-purpose flour with the addition of ⅓ ounce baking powder to 1 pound flour. I do not recommend its use. Different recipes require different proportions of baking powder to flour. If the flour is old, or if it has been kept in a damp place, the aerating properties of the baking powder will be adversely affected.

5. Gluten flour is strongly proteinaceous hard wheat flour that has had much of the starch washed out of it. It is handy to keep around. You can add a bit to all-purpose flour to bring it up to bread flour strength. Professional bakers always add gluten flour to those yeast breads that contain "heavy carriers" like raisins, nuts, and glacéed fruits. The extra strength imparted helps keep the objects in place within the dough so they do not settle to the bottom of the loaf.

Things to Remember

• You can know the protein content of any flour by looking at the labeling information on the side of the package. The percentage of protein indicates the gluten strength of the flour.

• During baking, flour loses 3 to 4 percentage points worth of protein. For health's sake it behooves us to select the highest protein strength available when we bake.

• There is a hand test to determine hard and soft flours. Soft starchy flour, when squeezed tightly in the hand, will hold together in a mass. Squeeze hard wheat flour and it will crumble to powder immediately as the hand is opened.

ON YEAST

For practical purposes, regular active dry yeast in packets was used throughout the testing of the recipes in this book. This is, however, the most expensive way to obtain dry yeast, which can be more economically bought in bulk at health food stores. (One tablespoon of yeast is equal to one packet of dry yeast.) Bulk yeast can last for months, refrigerated in a tightly sealed jar.

New, rapid-rising dry yeasts have recently appeared on the market, and they do indeed cut rising time by one third to one half, but I find there is a corresponding loss of pleasing yeast flavoring essence, and so recommend that these be used only in last-minute emergencies.

Fresh yeast is wonderful if you can get it. Bakeries will sometimes sell you a pound or so, but since less than an ounce is required in many recipes and it keeps for only about two weeks, it is far less practical than dry yeast in any but the most prolific home kitchens. It is slightly more potent and flavorful than dry yeast, but it oxidizes, turns dark, and loses its potency after a fortnight. One ounce of fresh yeast equals one packet dry yeast.

Despite many instructions to the contrary, it is no longer necessary to proof yeast. Proofing was done when refrigeration was not as reliable as it is today. Nor is it necessary to add sugar to dissolving yeast in order to give yeast something to feed on. You need only taste the intense sweetness of fresh green wheat kernels to know that there is plenty of natural convertible sugar in the wheat flour itself.

ON BUTTER

I prefer the taste of unsalted butter. Most recipes, especially those calling for a goodly quantity of butter, will specify unsalted. Occasionally those recipes needing only a tablespoon or two of the substance will just call for butter, in which case you can use whatever is at hand—it isn't necessary to run out to the store for unsalted butter if you don't have it.

However, when it comes to buttering bread, use the real thing. Sweet, unsalted creamery butter on fresh bread—nothing could taste finer.

ON KNEADING

The word *knead* is partly derived from the Old English word *cnotta*, or knot—a concept that seems to me particularly apt, for to knead is to tie together, to "knot" together with the hands, the disparate elements of seawater, fungus, and flour into a vital, intricately tangled creature.

In the process of kneading and knotting we exert ourselves; our energy and passion seemingly flow through our hands and transfer, almost mystically, life force into lumpen matter. There is no other foodstuff I can think of that is so dependent on the correct laying on of hands for its successful conception. If then our loaves do not rise sufficiently, if they are sodden and heavy in spirit, it is as if those loaves become a direct insult to our very being. Many a novice baker gives up after one or two baking attempts simply because the fragile ego cannot stand the affront of what seems to be simplicity itself gone wrong.

In kneading it is our job to develop the gluten protein of flour by moistening it with water and working it under the hands until it becomes firm and elastic. It is our job to disperse the molecules of fermenting yeast within this proteinaceous mass so that carbon dioxide passes evenly throughout the expanding loaf and ensures that our bread will not have bubbles and air pockets and oddly crumbed textures. The process is akin to a potter's "wedging" clay correctly before throwing a pot. If the clay is not kneaded before shaping, if minute molecules of air remain trapped in the clay, pots baked in the kiln will tend to blisters, lopsided proportions, and all manner of peculiarities.

To knead efficiently, place the dough on a counter of the correct height. You should be able to stand in comfortable shoes, with your arms angled slightly before you, your elbows unbent, and your palms pressed flat against the kneading surface. If the counter is too high, you will not be able to exert your full strength. If the counter is too low, your back will ache with the effort. Take off your rings. Turn on the radio. Flour the counter and place the dough smack on the flour. Stand with your right foot ahead of your left and lean into the dough with the weight on your right palm. Mush the dough forward with your right hand, then draw the dough back and over itself, again with the right hand. The left hand stabilizes the dough, gives the dough a quarter turn, and repositions it each time the right hand presses forward. You should exert great body force against the dough with each motion. You should exert your concentrated willpower on the dough, as well as your physical power. You should rhythmically knead for a good 10 minutes. At the end of this time in summer you should have developed a light sweat. In winter you should feel heated and self-satisfied. The dough should feel squeezable and have somewhat of a putty nature to it. It should be firm, and dry enough not to stick to the palms. It should respond to a testing pinch with a small contraction and then a gentle, visible, responsive sigh of immediate relaxation.

ON TOOLS

The only tools you really need for bread making are a bowl, a work surface, and a pair of strong hands. I have never been enamored of mixing machines and dough hook attachments, for I find that only small amounts of dough can be kneaded effectively in such machines, and during kneading the dough sticks to the hook and the machine needs to be stopped a distressing number of times to rectify the situation.

PANS

I rarely recommend a particular size pan in any of my recipes, because the process of baking bread is so variable that you should really simply follow your good sense rather than a precise direction. In general, when using a loaf pan fill the pan two thirds full of dough and you will have a nice, plump loaf.

Keep on hand standard loaf pans made of metal and glass, the standard sizes being 9 x 5 x 3 inches and 8 x 4 x 3 inches. At times you may find that you can make two small loaves instead of one large loaf or vice versa. Also have large pizza pans and baking sheets for spectacular big loaves.

BREAD KNIVES

I recommend the purchase of a good bread knife, because a serrated knife edge cuts bread neatly without tearing it.

Many of the breads in this book can simply be pulled apart by hand —my favorite method of breaking bread.

BOWLS

You will need two or three bowls; large, 5-quart sizes are the most useful. A handsome antique ceramic bowl, always used for bread rising, is a nice traditional and ritual object to invest in, use, and hand down within the family.

SMALL UTENSILS

Have also wooden spoons of various sizes, a dough scraper (a heavy stainless steel model is sturdier than the wood-handled number), and a plant mister to add sprays of moisture to the oven while bread is baking. Have straight-edged razor blades for slitting dough surfaces, a pastry brush, and a mortar and pestle.

ON BASKET BREADS

There is a series of tucks, pleats, and folds that professional bakers use to incorporate the tension necessary to allow dough to remain firmly rounded as they form circular shapes, particularly baguettes and plump country loaves. Without these manipulations, dough that is shaped by hand into a round and plopped onto a baking tray to rise soon loses its ductile strength and spreads into a flat circle. Much to the dismay of the bread maker, no amount of prodding or shoring up will return the dough to its former spherelike shape.

For a home baker, it has always seemed to me more reasonable to allow the bread to rise in baskets and depend on the baskets' structured molding forms to impart strong tensile shapes. Those shapes come about when once-risen dough is placed in a heavily floured canvas-lined basket. The dough then rises a second time in the basket. It expands to the edge of the basket and rises up the sides. Air circulates through the loosely woven basket and canvas, and a thin strong skin forms over the surface of the dough. When the dough has risen sufficiently, the basket is turned over and the dough is gently reversed onto a baking pan. The dough receives another brief rise to allow it to regain the expansion it had before the reversal knocked the wind out of it. Before the bread goes into the oven, slashes (*coups de lame*) are made just through the top crust. These allow carbon dioxide to escape in an orderly manner and therefore the bread to bake in an even shape.

There should be no baguettes puffed on one side; no round country loaf that cracks and spreads unattractively.

Making a basket mold is a relatively simple matter, and the basket becomes a handsome kitchen ornament as well. Choose some long baskets in which to make baguettes and a variety of round baskets 10 to 15 inches in diameter. All baskets should be about 3 inches tall and have slightly sloping sides. Buy enough canvas or coarsely woven cotton to line the baskets. Cut shapes of cloth and insert them in the baskets. Using thin white kitchen string or heavy rug thread, sew the material into the baskets. You can use a whipstitch over the rim of the basket, or just pass the needle in and out between the basket's warp and weave. Tack the material down in several places on the bottom of the basket. It is not necessary to do world-class sewing here.

Each time before bread is to be formed, place a good quantity of flour in the basket and shake the basket about until the flour spreads into an even ⅛-inch-thick layer on bottom and sides. In time the basket will retain a permanent encrustation of flour. A bit of mold may even form if you are lucky. The taste of the most famous bread in Paris (Poilaine's) is alleged to be highly affected by the natural molds found in that firm's ancient shaping baskets.

SPECIAL BAKERS' FINISHES

One of the greatest delights in bread making is the first glimpse of the finished baked goods. No matter how perfectly bread was formed by hand, how carefully the dough was rounded and smoothed, the final loaf appears bearing its own willful personality. There are clefts and crevices, fine networks of crackled crust, small complexities of bubbles and blisters randomly present on the surface, none of which were planned for but all of which add to the unique appearance of that loaf and testify to its handmade, homemade individuality.

Unlike professional bakers, who try for uniformity of product and automatically reject any loaf that falls too far from the established norm, the home baker should strive for ways in which to make his or her loaf handsomely rustic. I personally adore the surfaces of French *pain de campagne*, those rough country loaves sold in every *boulangerie*, and I've tried always to emulate their appearance. It is not possible or even desirable to have complete control over the visual aspects of bread making, but I will describe here some of the techniques and finishes that are possible for experimentation.

BASKET BREAD WITH GUARANTEED CREVICES
(Color plate 2)

It is easiest to arrive at a creviced look by forming bread in a basket. (See "On Basket Breads.") The idea here is to put a goodly amount of dough in a basket that is just slightly too small to hold it, so that its expansion becomes cramped. You can flour the basket if a crackled white finish is desired, or leave the basket unfloured. (If you do not have a lined basket, you can improvise by draping a dish towel in a basket and getting a plain, unfloured surface.) Put the dough in the basket, cover lightly with a towel, and let the dough rise for 1 hour. Remove the towel from the top of the basket and place a lightly oiled baking sheet over the basket. Reverse the basket and baking sheet together and let the dough drop onto the baking sheet. The dough will have been held in the basket with such tension that, when freed, it will expand before your eyes. The thin crust that has dried over the surface will stretch and split apart in two or three places, forming crevices. If the dough rested in a floured basket, the adhering white crust will shatter into a fine etching of broken flour.

BASKET BREAD WITH SCORCHED DESIGN
(Color plate 1)

To scorch a pattern onto a surface, you must first cover the loaf with an even layer of white flour. The dough should be in a basket that will not cramp its expansion. I use a large, 15-inch cloth-lined basket for this bread, and I make a large flat loaf so that there will be a good amount of surface to be decorated.

Put a layer of flour in the basket and give the basket a shake or two on the counter so that the flour settles evenly. The layer should be a good ¼ inch thick. Flatten the dough with your hands and put it in the basket. Let the dough rise, then turn it out onto an oiled baking sheet. Be as gentle as possible with the dough so as not to disturb the adhering flour. Give the dough a short rise, then bake the loaf in the oven. When the loaf has finished baking, it will be ready to scorch. I use an old knife-sharpening steel for my scorching utensil, but I've also improvised with a heavy metal skewer and several lengths of coat hanger wire twisted together. Heat your scorching utensil on a burner or directly over a flame until it is very hot. Place the utensil on the surface of the loaf, and if it is hot enough, it should leave a dense scorched line embedded in the flour. (There will be a certain amount of acrid smell and smoke with this process.) Quickly move the utensil an inch or so away from the first line and try to scorch a second and a third line on the surface. You will have to repeat the heating process several times before the entire loaf will be covered. You can make a series of parallel lines; or a diamond crisscross; or several intersecting lines that dissect the loaf into wedges.

A LIGHT TOPPING FOR A DARK LOAF
(Color plate 4)

A good finish for a dark-grain loaf (rye, Russian bread, pumpernickel, etc.) is a light-colored topping that drips and runs at intervals down the surface of the loaf. This is most effectively done with a plump round loaf.

To make the topping, put ½ teaspoon yeast and ⅓ cup all-purpose flour in a bowl. Stirring all the while, add a small stream of warm water to the flour. Add only enough to make a thick, gravylike consistency. The topping should drop heavily, sluggishly, off a spoon.

Just before the dark loaf is put in the oven to bake, half spoon/half pour the topping over the top center. You should be able to control the drips down the sides and their placement if the topping is of the correct thickness. Bake the loaf and keep an eye on it. If, after 30 minutes, the light topping looks as if it might begin to brown, put a piece of aluminum foil over the top to keep the surface white.

THE JACKSON POLLOCK SPLATTER FINISH
(Color plate 3)

A nice finish for any kind of loaf, white bread or dark, is the variegated, streaked look that results from using a topping with oil in it. In a bowl combine 1 egg yolk, 2 tablespoons water, 2 tablespoons oil, and 1 teaspoon yeast. Stir and let sit for 10 minutes. Add 2 tablespoons flour and 2 tablespoons cornstarch and then, stirring all the while, add enough water to bring the topping to a thin texture approaching light gravy.

Just before the loaf goes into the oven, brush, dab, and dribble the topping over the surface.

HIGH ALTITUDE BAKING

High altitudes and atmospheric conditions play a role in how dough rises and behaves in the oven. In the case of high altitude baking, it is simply a matter of keeping an eye on the rising dough. Gas expands more quickly at lofty altitudes, and it will therefore be ready for baking 10, perhaps 15, minutes sooner than usual. Do not change ingredients or baking time in any recipe— just keep a close eye on the dough. As the air is dryer at high altitudes, it is also helpful to spray the oven frequently with a plant mister during the baking period and to put a pan of steaming water under the baking loaf.

At mountainous altitudes, baking powder breads tend to rise slightly higher. If they are baked too slowly, the dough can spill out of the pan. It is a good idea to increase the temperature slightly, say 25°, to assure that the bread sets quickly and firmly.

If the weather is cool, dough will take longer to rise. It can be nudged along in a slightly warmed oven. If the weather is moist and warm, yeast dough will rise in record time. Bake it sooner than you normally would.

MISCELLANEOUS THOUGHTS ON BREAD

The following are a few notes or thoughts about situations or problems that may come up in the bread-making process. Some of them are my personal preferences; some are tips I've found useful over my years as a baker.

TIPS ON PREPARING SPECIAL DOUGHS

Add a bit of gluten flour to bread containing heavy carriers (a bakers' term for raisins, nuts, glacéed fruits, etc.). This will add strength to the dough and keep the heavy objects from falling to the bottom of the loaf.

The more elements contained in the bread dough (other than flour, water, yeast, and salt), the lower the baking temperature should be and the higher the gluten content of the flour should be. The lighter and yeastier the dough, the higher the baking temperature can be.

Breads that depend on baking powder for their aeration should be assembled, mixed, and put to bake rapidly. Don't overwork them.

A NOTE ABOUT RISING

When bread is given its last rising, look for an expanded volume of dough that is 90 percent of the final volume of the loaf. Depend on your oven only for the last 10 percent of the loaf's volume. Bakers call this "oven push."

THOUGHTS ON BAKING

Breads were traditionally baked on stone hearths in wood-fired ovens. The risen loaf would be placed on a flat "pele" (a sort of flattened shovel), lifted into the oven, and, with a quick releasing movement, dropped onto the oven floor. As the bread baked, the oven temperature would slowly fall.

I have experimented with dropping temperatures in my ovens, and find the technique effective for large loaves. It produces a crisp crust and chewy crumb. Start the bread in a 400°F oven; drop the temperature to 375°F after 5 minutes; then drop it again to 350°F after 10 minutes. Turn the oven off 10 minutes before the bread needs to come out.

Use a plant mister to inject a little steam into your oven to ensure crisp crusts. Spray the oven and the loaf generously several times during the first 15 to 20 minutes of baking. I prefer this method to the traditional tip of setting a baking pan of water on the bottom of the oven, which usually seems to be of little effect. (At times, however, I combine both methods.)

To test a bread for doneness, open the oven, slide out the baking pan, lift up the bread, and give the bottom a good knock with your fist. The sound should be resonant and hollow, a sort of dull thump that is indicative of air—as opposed to moisture—inside the bread. A wetness, a heaviness, a sense of steam given off under the center of the loaf or condensed on the pan immediately under the loaf suggest that more baking time is desirable.

If the crust seems too crisp and heavy when bread comes from the oven, wrap the loaf in a towel and briefly leave it to cool. The loaf will be trapped in its own escaping moisture and the crust will soften.

If your loaf turns out "ropy"—that is, wet and dense, with small strings or "ropes" of wet dough running through the crumb—ask yourself the following questions:

Was the dough sufficiently kneaded? If not, the protein in the dough was not sufficiently developed, the gluten did not firm up adequately, and the multitude of gas particles necessary to expand and leaven the bread were not trapped evenly throughout the dough. The dough sat heavy and unlifted during baking.

Was the rising time cut short? If so, even if the dough was correctly kneaded, the fermenting gases did not have time to expand the dough mass, so the baked loaf seems underdone.

Was the oven temperature too high? If so, the exterior of the loaf hardened quickly, and even though the dough was sufficiently kneaded and the rising time was generous, the expanding gases were trapped under the crust. The baked loaf, when cut into, will be dolorously inert.

A TIP ON CLEANING UP

The best way to clean up a dough-encrusted counter is to scrape it first with a metal pastry scraper. Get up as much of the dough as possible, then wet a plastic scrub pad and use it to remove the remaining fine particles. Don't attack the mess with a sponge.

USING LEFTOVERS

Don't let an overabundance of bread go to waste. If bread is going stale, try the following:

Cut bread into ½-inch slices. Cut out rounds 2 or 3 inches in diameter and leave to dry in the open air or in a warm oven. Store in an airtight container. These rounds can be used *"tremper la soupe,"* an odd little French expression that means literally "to soak the soup" —that is, to put rounds of dried bread in a bowl, pour soup over the bread, and allow the bread to soak and disperse into the soup, thereby adding body to the broth.

Make both fine and coarse crumbs. As bread is drying, break it into portions and grind in a blender or food processor. Put the crumbs in a sieve and shake out all the very fine particles. Rub more through the sieve. Let the crumbs dry completely, then store fine crumbs in one jar, coarse crumbs in another. The fine crumbs can be used for breading veal cutlets and the like; the coarse crumbs can be mixed with grated cheese and used on gratin surfaces.

STORING BREAD

Ideally, homemade bread should be eaten very fresh. After you remove bread from the oven, take it out of or off the pan, set the loaf on a rack, and let it cool. If bread is to be stored, either put it in a breadbox, or store it in a plastic bag or tightly bound plastic wrap in the refrigerator. Plain white and grain breads keep 2 to 5 days; sweet breads tend to last a bit longer.

I prefer not to freeze plain yeasted breads. Baking powder breads do freeze well, however, and sometimes their flavors even seem to improve after freezing. To freeze breads, let them cool completely, wrap loaves first in plastic wrap and again in foil, then seal them in a plastic bag. Label each bread with its name and the date on which it was frozen.

To thaw, bring the bread to room temperature, then warm it in a moderate (300°F) oven for about 15 minutes for a large loaf, 8 to 10 minutes for rolls or muffins.

The
RECIPES

VARIATIONS ON BASIC BREAD

All life moving to one measure—daily bread.
Wilfrid Wilson Gibson

Basic white bread, that most useful of all breads, can appear in a variety of guises: shaped and formed into wondrous heads of wheat and hearts and flowers; flavored with a potent sour dough or cornmeal-leavened starter; stretched thin and pulled out into crisp, crackling *ciabatta*; twisted into a giant salty pretzel; teased into a honeycombed fretwork; colored and swirled with spinach and tomatoes; stuffed with an abundance of eggs and sausage, olives and cheese—the possibilities are endless.

Try Grandmother's Loaf with a Crackling Crust for a nostalgic breakfast, or the World's Largest Hamburger Bun for a children's party. For those with an artistic bent, there is the classic *L'Artichaut* from France, or a handsome cauliflower loaf formed from dark and light doughs in variegated patterns.

Basic White Bread

The bread that is most useful in life, that best acts as a complement to sandwiches, cheeses, and meals, is plain white bread. By "plain" I mean a bread that is created from the barest essentials necessary for a yeasted loaf—salt, water, yeast, and flour. (Incidentally, these four elements are the only ones legally permitted in France's basic white breads and baguettes.) Gone are the fats, the powdered eggs and milk, the sugars, the preservatives so frequently found in commercial breads. Gone are all those components that turn bread to airy sponges or densely crumbed cakes or borderline sweets. What is left is simplicity itself—the essence of grain seasoned with salt and yeastily uplifted into the "staff of life."

The following recipes are for the most basic of loaves. For the sake of convenience, there are five formulations for the same recipe, each progressively larger in bulk, so that all shapes are possible, from standard 9 x 5 x 3-inch loaves to larger free-form breads. Generally speaking, 1 cup water and 2¾ cups flour will work up to a satisfactory dough, but I have seen this flour amount vary by ½ cup, depending on weather conditions or the age of the flour. The final amount of flour necessary to make a fine, elastic, nonsticky dough should be arrived at by feel.

Formula 1

Fills 1 standard loaf pan

1 package yeast
1½ cups warm water
1¼ teaspoons salt
Scant 4¼ cups unbleached flour

Formula 2

Makes 2 small round breads or 1
  large round basket bread

1 package yeast
2 cups warm water
1½ teaspoons salt
5½ cups unbleached flour

Formula 3

Makes 2 medium rounds or fills 2
  loaf pans

1 package plus 1 teaspoon yeast
2½ cups warm water
2 teaspoons salt
Generous 6¾ cups unbleached
  flour

Formula 4

Makes 2 large rounds or fills 2
  loaf pans

1 package plus 1½ teaspoons
  yeast
3 cups warm water
2½ teaspoons salt
8¼ cups unbleached flour

Formula 5

Makes large shaped loaves
  needing a lot of oven space, or
  1 large round and 1 medium-
  shaped round, or fills 3 loaf
  pans

2 packages yeast
3½ cups warm water
1 tablespoon salt
10 cups unbleached flour

Dissolve the yeast in warm water. Stir in the salt, then add enough of the flour so that the dough can be turned out onto a kneading surface. Knead, adding more flour as necessary, until the dough no longer feels sticky. (The palm of your hand pressed into the center of the dough should come away clean, with no sense of "pull" involved, and certainly no dough should cling to your hand.) Knead the dough vigorously for 10 minutes.

Put the dough in a clean oiled bowl, cover with a towel, set the bowl in a warm spot, and let the dough rise. When it has doubled in bulk (usually in 1 hour), form it into whatever shape you desire, and let the dough rise again. Bake in a preheated 350°F oven. (Professional bakers look for 85 to 90 percent of the loaf's expansion to occur during the rising stage, with only a final 10 to 15 percent expansion during baking.)

Bake the loaf or loaves until they sound very hollow when rapped firmly underneath with your knuckles.

SPECIAL SHAPED BREADS

It is possible, of course, to shape bread into any imaginable form, and appropriately shaped breads are splendid surprises to honor special occasions. The four "shaped breads" that follow seem to me particularly useful, in that their forms follow their functions. The first two are good pull-apart loaves; the second two are large solid loaves that can serve as centerpieces or be hollowed and filled with various dips.

The Bunch of Grapes

(Color plate 5)

Make Formula 4 or 5 of Basic White Bread (page 25). After the dough has risen, pinch off egg-sized portions of dough (approximately 30 to 35 portions). Form one portion into a rough ball, then smooth the ball by placing it atop the index and middle fingers of your right hand. Gently smooth the dough with the thumb and index finger of your left hand. When the top of the ball is satin-smooth, lift off the dough and squeeze it together at the bottom by contracting the left thumb and forefinger so that they both lift and almost pinch off the perfect ball of dough. Make 26 to 31 perfect "grapes," then arrange them in a cluster on an oiled baking sheet. (Do not pile them on top of one another.)

Stretch out one dough portion and form a rough stem. Tuck it under the top middle of the bread and stretch and shape it to one side. Roll one portion into a long, thin coil. Curl the coil like a tendril over the grapes. Combine the remaining two portions of dough and roll them out to a circle. Stretch the circle to make a rough triangle. Using a knife, cut several notches in the dough and drape it like a leaf near the stem. Brush dough with a glaze made from *1 egg yolk beaten with 2 teaspoons water.* Allow the "grapes" to rise for 30 minutes, or until all the spaces between them have filled with expanded dough and the cluster looks full. Bake in a preheated 350°F oven for around 45 minutes, or until the loaf sounds hollow when tapped on the bottom.

This is an excellent bread to serve for summer meals or at a wine and cheese tasting.

Have-a-Heart Loaf

This loaf seems to me the epitome of comforting, companionable bread meant to be broken together. Make Formula 3 or 4 of Basic White Bread (page 25). Let the bread rise, then take it from the bowl, hold the dough with both hands, and shake and stretch it until it droops and sags into a rough triangle. Lay the triangle on a large oiled baking sheet. Press and shape the dough until it forms a large heart. Make cuts through the dough as shown in drawing at top. Shape and compact the dough at the cut marks until large open spaces are formed and the final pattern looks like the second drawing. Brush the loaf with a glaze made from *1 egg yolk beaten with 2 teaspoons water.* Let the bread rise for 30 minutes, then bake in a preheated 350°F oven for around 40 to 45 minutes, or until the loaf sounds hollow when tapped on the bottom.

The Wheaten Loaf

(Color plate 7)

This loaf is formed in a classic Italian bread shape, one that vaguely resembles an overblown head of wheat. Make Formula 3, 4, or 5 of Basic White Bread (page 25), and add a bit of extra flour so that the dough is quite stiff. Let the dough rise, then remove it from the bowl and place it on a large oiled baking sheet. Shape the dough into a long fat cylinder, then create a point at each end. Let the dough rise in a warm spot for 30 minutes. Brush it with a glaze made from *1 egg yolk beaten with 2 teaspoons water.* Using a single-edged razor blade, make a slash or ridge ½ inch deep into the dough, about 2 inches from the outside edge of the bread. Make a second ridge parallel to the first.

Using scissors, make cuts around the edge of the bread, 2 inches apart and extending to the first ridge. Gently spread and point the cut portions.

Let the bread rise for another 10 to 15 minutes. Bake in a preheated 350°F oven for around 1 hour, or until the bread sounds hollow when tapped on the bottom.

The Starfish

(Color plate 8)

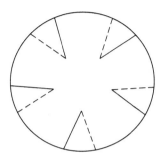

This loaf can be made large or small. It is particularly effective when it is large, hollowed, and filled with a seafood dip.

Make a batch of Basic White Bread (page 25) of the desired volume and let it rise once. Remove the dough from the bowl, shape it into a ball, and place on a large oiled baking sheet or pizza pan. Flatten the ball and, using a rolling pin, taper the outside rim of the circle until it is about ½ inch thick, while leaving the center of the circle as full and plump as possible.

With a sharp knife, make 5 evenly spaced cuts two thirds of the way into the dough. Trim off and remove the small wedge of dough at each cut. Press the cut-out portions together into a ball and slide it under the middle of the dough, to add height and thickness at the center. Tuck the dough under at the end of each of the cut portions so that it resembles the point of a star. Pinch up a ½-inch-tall ridge of dough from each point to the top center of the star. Press the sharp end of a round pastry nozzle all over the surface of the bread (except for the ridges), so that the exterior is textured like a starfish.

Let the dough rise for 30 to 40 minutes. If it rises unevenly, make some gentle cosmetic tucks before putting the bread in the oven. Glaze the loaf with *1 egg yolk beaten with 1 teaspoon soy sauce and 1 teaspoon water.* (The soy sauce "antiques" the impressed design.)

Bake in a preheated 350°F oven for 1 hour, or until the bread sounds hollow when tapped on the bottom.

Sunflower Bread

Makes 1 large sunflower
(Color plate 9)

1½ packages yeast
3 cups warm water
3 teaspoons salt
¼ cup lightly toasted sunflower
  seeds, pulverized to a near
  flour in a blender or food
  processor
About 7¾ cups unbleached flour

For the glaze
1 egg yolk beaten with 2
  teaspoons water

About 4 tablespoons poppy seeds
Large pinch turmeric or
  powdered saffron

Dissolve the yeast in water. Add the salt and sunflower seeds. Stir in flour until a dough thick enough to knead results. Turn the dough out onto a floured surface and continue working in additional flour and kneading until the dough is firm and elastic (about 12 minutes). Put the dough in an oiled bowl, oil the surface of the dough, and cover with a towel. Let rise in a warm spot for 1 hour. Oil a large baking sheet or pizza pan.

Remove the dough from the bowl, put it on the pan, and flatten it down. Roll the dough into a circle 13 to 14 inches in diameter. Try to leave the center thicker, the rim thinner. Press an inverted bowl about 8 inches in diameter into the center of the dough to leave a circular impression. Brush the 8-inch center with egg yolk glaze. Cover the center with a solid layer of poppy seeds. This will be the center of the sunflower.

To create "petals," with a sharp knife make cuts from the edge of the circle out to the rim of the dough at ¾-inch intervals. Gently round the outer end of each petal by tucking corners under. Lift and curl a few petals, and overlap them here and there. Add the turmeric or saffron to the remaining egg glaze to yellow it, then brush over the petals. Let rise for 20 minutes. Preheat the oven to 350°F.

Bake for 35 to 40 minutes, or until the petals are golden. Let guests break off portions.

ON *PAIN AU LEVAIN,* OR SOURDOUGH BREAD

Pain au levain is not, as its name might suggest, merely yeasted bread. The *levain* refers to a portion of soured dough that is saved from the batch at each baking session, then used to impart its flavor and leavening qualities to the subsequent mass of new dough. Visually, *pain au levain* is the quintessence of a comforting loaf, for it is formed in large inviting rounds, its surface a composition of flour-dusted furrows and razor-slit clefts. (The look-alike loaves in French *boulangeries* made with unsoured *levains* are called *pain de campagne*, "country bread.")

Its ingredients are few and simple: water, salt, flours, a sourdough *levain*, and, frequently, more yeast. It is by regulating the strength of the *levain* and choosing the flours and their mix that the best-known of French bakers (such as M. Poilaine in Paris) achieve the very personal loaves for which their bakeries are famous. In the same way at home, you can determine texture, flavor, and color of bread crumb through experimentation, and in turn develop truly individual loaves that are a pleasure to eat as well as to look at.

Pain au levain is dependent for its slightly soured flavor on a *levain* that also is soured, and to propagate this *levain* it is necessary to have a sourdough starter. The simplest way to come by a starter is either to be given 2 cups' worth of sourdough (which is, in effect, already a *levain*) by someone, or to buy a dry sourdough starter mix at a specialty food shop. Simply follow the package directions to activate the starter and wait the designated time for the culture to become sufficiently soured. On the night before you bake your bread, build a "sponge" by adding flour and water to the starter; next day, bottle half the mixture as *levain* and refrigerate it to await the next baking session.

In a bakery, formulating and dividing the *levain* is a daily procedure, which allows the baker to have firm control over the degree to which the breads taste of sourness. In the home, however, where bread is baked less frequently, the *levain* can grow powerfully acerbic when left overlong and unused, but by no means should you feel a slave to a starter, or to the demand on its package that it be used every week. In the home, it is perhaps easier to think of the *levain* merely as a flavoring element rather than as the active yeasting agent within the bread. The *levain* will become less of a tyrant, and with this in mind, you can use the *levain* plus additional yeast at every baking. In fact, most bakeries follow this procedure of adding yeast to the *levain*, because although their very active *levains* may indeed raise the dough mass in time, they take too long to be commercially practical.

At various times I have done all of the following with my *levain*, with no ill effect on its flavoring properties:

1. Added beer to the sponge to increase the sourness of the *levain*.
2. Left it for three weeks, poured off the pungent liquid floating on

top after the hiatus, and replaced the liquid with water, a bit of yeast, and a pinch of sugar.
3. Intensified the flavor by adding malt and mixed grains.
4. Lifted off the top crust and thrown half of the *levain* away.
5. Loaned it to friends during my vacation.

The point of all this is that a *levain* can be easier to keep and maintain than most of the packaged starter directions suggest, *so long as* the home baker views it primarily as a flavor enhancer whose degree of sourness can be intensified or decreased.

Sourdough Bread (*Pain au Levain*)

Makes 1 large loaf
(Color plate 6)

For the sponge
2 cups sourdough starter (*levain*)
1 cup lukewarm water
1¼ cups unbleached flour

For the bread
1 package yeast
1½ cups warm water
2 tablespoons rye flour

1 tablespoon buckwheat flour (optional)
1 tablespoon ground toasted sesame seeds
1 tablespoon bran
1 tablespoon malt (optional)
2 teaspoons salt
About 5 to 5½ cups unbleached flour

To make the sponge, empty the starter into a mixing bowl. Stir in lukewarm water and then the flour. Cover the sponge with a towel, place in a warm spot (in a pilot-lighted oven, near a heat register, etc.), and leave for 24 to 36 hours. At the end of this time, stir down the sponge and put half of it back in its container to act as *levain* for your next baking.

To make bread, dissolve the yeast in warm water. Stir the dissolved yeast into the sponge and add the rye flour, buckwheat flour, seeds, bran, malt, and salt. Add enough unbleached flour to form a soft dough, then turn the mass out onto a floured work surface and start kneading. Sprinkle flour on the surface as necessary and work the dough for a good 12 minutes, until it feels firm and elastic. Add only the minimum of flour needed, and keep in mind that the dough should remain malleable and soft enough to form easily. Don't bind it into a difficult-to-work lump.

Put the dough in a clean, lightly oiled bowl, cover it with a kitchen towel, and let it rise until doubled in bulk. (If time is not pressing, it is good to let the dough have a leisurely rising period and more time to develop its sourness. Try giving it 2 to 3 hours in a cool room.) When the dough has risen enough, remove it from the bowl, punch down, and shape into a round. (The bread could also be formed in a basket, if you so desire. See page 13).

Let the formed loaf rise, towel-covered, in a warm place until it has reached almost full size. (Again, a longer rising in a cool spot will more fully develop the flavor.) With a razor, make surface slits, 2 across and 2 down, as in a tic-tac-toe grid.

Bake the bread in a preheated 350°F oven for 1 hour. Test doneness by turning the baked loaf over and knocking on its bottom with a fist to see if it sounds hollow.

Remove the bread from the oven and let it cool, propped at a tilt or on a cake rack so the bottom crust does not become moist and soft. *Pain au levain* should have a good crisp crust.

Rapid Sourdough Baguettes

Makes two 27-inch-long baguettes

1 package yeast
1¼ cups warm water
½ cup sourdough starter
3¾ cups unbleached flour
1½ teaspoons salt
2 teaspoons red wine vinegar

For the glaze
1 teaspoon salt dissolved in 2 tablespoons water

Dissolve the yeast in warm water. Add the sourdough starter and stir well. Stir in 2½ cups flour and let the mixture stand, covered with a towel and in a warm spot, for 30 minutes.

Stir down and put ½ cup of the sponge mixture back in the sourdough starter jar.

Add salt and vinegar to the sponge. Stir in the remaining 1¼ cups flour. Work the dough well with your hands (it is quite sticky). Knead it; stretch it between your hands; pummel it on a lightly floured surface; work vigorously for 10 minutes to toughen the gluten. Put the dough in a clean oiled bowl. Cover it with a towel and let it rise in a warm spot for 1 hour.

Lightly oil a baguette pan. Divide the dough in two, and elongate each portion to fit a baguette impression. Let rise for 35 minutes. Brush tops with salt water glaze.

This is a rapid baguette recipe I make when I want a sourdough flavor in a bread but have not had time to let a starter dough develop overnight. This recipe is devised for a metal double baguette pan 27½ inches long, the style most frequently available in kitchen equipment stores. You might also form this as one longer, wider loaf in a basket (see "On Basket Breads," page 13).

Put a pan of hot water on the bottom of the oven. Preheat the oven to 350°F.

Bake the baguettes for 20 minutes. If you have a plant mister, quickly spray water into the oven and over the loaves two or three times during baking. Turn the baguettes over in the pans and let them bake for another 10 minutes (30 minutes in all).

Ciabatta

Makes 1 loaf
(Color plate 10)

The Italian word ciabatta *literally means "down-at-heel" or an old broken shoe or slipper, but the bread named* ciabatta *is figuratively meant to represent the "heel" of boot-shaped Italy, the province of Apulia. The bread is long—as long as you can make it in your oven—and it has a short baking time, a delectable crisp crust, and a most unusual kneading procedure.*

2 tablespoons olive oil
1 envelope yeast
2 cups warm water

2 teaspoons salt
4½ cups unbleached flour

Generously oil a bowl with the 2 tablespoons of olive oil and set aside.

Dissolve the yeast in warm water. Add the salt and stir until dissolved. Stir in 4 cups flour and mix until smooth. The dough will be very wet. If you have a heavy, sturdy mixer with a dough hook, you can put the dough to knead on the machine for 8 minutes.

Kneading by hand, scoop up the dough with your hands, make fists, then work it by twisting your hands and arms around and around each other, pulling and stretching the dough back and forth much like an accordion player. (This is very good exercise for the upper arms.) Keep at it until the dough feels firmer (it will still be wet) and elastic, around 10 minutes. Scrape the dough from your hands and put it in the oiled bowl. Cover and let rise in a warm place for 1 hour.

Set a baking pan filled with warm water on the bottom rack of the oven. Preheat the oven to 400°F. Choose the longest baking sheet that will fit in your oven. (You can even overlap two rimless baking sheets, if you wish.) Oil the baking sheet.

My *ciabatta* is 22 inches long and 5 or 6 inches wide. Yours might be no longer than 15 inches and comparatively wider. Thickly sprinkle ½ cup flour along a work surface in an area the length of your proposed bread. Lift the dough from the bowl, stretch it out to the desired length, and immediately put it down in the flour. (If a thin crust has formed on top of the dough, be sure to place that interesting torn-crust side down in the flour.) Stretch and pull the dough out with your fingers; it should be no thicker than ¾ inch at any point. Transfer the dough, flour side up, to the oiled baking sheet. The surface should be a textured vista of nubs and crevices. Square up the corners, and stretch out any dough that is too thick. Let the dough rise for 15 minutes.

Bake for 30 to 35 minutes. If you have a plant mister, spray water into the oven and around (but not on) the bread several times. Serve warm and crackling.

Pretzel Bread

Makes 3 breads

1½ packages yeast
2 teaspoons sugar
2 cups warm water
2 tablespoons plus 2 teaspoons
   salt
About 4 cups bread flour
Cornmeal
2 tablespoons baking soda

For the glaze
2 tablespoons baking soda
1 egg yolk beaten with 2
   teaspoons water

For the topping
Coarse salt to taste

From this recipe you will get three marvelous, oversized, pretzel-shaped breads. Poaching the breads in steaming water guarantees their chewy crumb and thin crisp crusts.

Dissolve the yeast and sugar in warm water. Stir in 2 teaspoons salt and 3 cups bread flour. Knead the dough together, then turn it out onto a floured counter and continue kneading and adding flour until a medium-firm mass evolves. Continue kneading in a firm and energetic manner; a good 12 minutes will ensure good gluten development. Put the dough in an oiled bowl, cover with a towel, and set aside to rise in a warm spot for 1 hour.

Divide the dough into 3 portions. Roll each portion back and forth under your palms to form a stretch of dough around 3 feet long. Scatter a dusting of cornmeal over a baking sheet. Lift each dough portion and twist it into a pretzel shape directly on the baking pan (see drawing). Moisten the ends of the pretzel with water and press them firmly together so they will adhere. Let the breads rise, uncovered, for around 30 minutes, or until they look like almost fully risen breads. As the breads are rising, put a large (10-inch diameter) pot half filled with water on the stove and bring it to a boil; reduce to a simmer. The breads should be rising next to the water so the steam helps proof them.

Preheat the oven to 350°F.

When the breads have risen, lower the water temperature so it is steaming but there is no agitation on the surface. Add the baking soda and 2 tablespoons salt to the water. Place two spatulas under one of the breads and lower the bread into the water. Let the bread poach for 1 minute, spooning water over its top crust once or twice. Use the spatulas to gently lift the bread and transfer it to an oiled baking tray. Poach the remaining breads.

Brush the breads with egg yolk glaze, and scatter coarse salt on top. It may be necessary to gently press the loaves back into shape.

Bake in the oven for 35 to 40 minutes. The breads should be golden brown, and their crusts should crackle crisply when pressed.

Honeycomb Loaf

Honeycomb Loaf is a handsome bread that is quickly baked and easily broken apart and shared at table. It also makes a spectacular addition on those occasions when a variety of breads are needed for display.

Makes 1 large loaf
(Color plate 12)

1 package yeast	**For the glaze**
1 tablespoon honey	4 tablespoons cornstarch
2 cups warm water	1 teaspoon yeast
2 teaspoons salt	1 tablespoon flour
About 5½ cups unbleached flour	About 2½ tablespoons water

Dissolve the yeast and honey in warm water. Add salt, then work in enough flour so that the dough can be turned out onto a work surface. Knead for 10 minutes, adding flour as necessary, until a firm, elastic dough results. Put the dough in a clean oiled bowl, cover with a towel, and set aside in a warm place to rise for 1 hour.

Oil the largest baking sheet that will fit in your oven. (If necessary, two flat-sided trays may be overlapped.)

Remove the dough from the bowl, place it on the baking sheet, and pat and stretch it out until it is a rough rectangle about ¾ inch thick. Using a 2½- to 3-inch round cookie cutter (temporarily bent out of shape so that it more nearly resembles the five-sided pentagon on which honeycomb is built), cut out plugs of dough, leaving inch-wide strips of dough between the cutouts. When the surface is "honeycombed," take the cut-out plugs and attach them under the outside edges wherever they can fit. Continue cutting and patching until the entire tray is full of dough. Tuck remaining dough portions under any of the attaching strips that might seem thin. Let the dough rise for 15 minutes.

Preheat the oven to 350°F.

To make the glaze, mix the cornstarch, yeast, and flour. Add enough water so that a paste results that is spreadable but not so thin that it will drip. Gently dab the glaze over the dough with a pastry brush. Put

Plate 7 (top left). The Wheaten Loaf; Plate 8 (top right). The Starfish; Plate 9. The Sunflower Bread. All of these breads are amusing forms of Basic White Bread.

Plate 10. *Classic Baguettes and Ciabatta in an antique French baguette basket.*

the bread in the oven and bake for around 30 minutes, or until the bread is golden brown and the top looks rustic. Let cool briefly before removing bread from tray.

Serve fresh and let guests break off portions as needed.

Boiling Beer Bread

Makes 1 loaf

Around 4 cups unbleached flour
½ cup beer (opened and staled for 24 hours)
1 cup warm water
1½ packages yeast
2 teaspoons salt

For the glaze
1 egg yolk beaten with 2 teaspoons of water

This loaf is moist and dense, rather like a Russian black bread in consistency, but of course it is a white loaf. It can be sliced ultrathin, and thus is an excellent choice for melba toast, canapés, and the like. Be sure to open the beer ahead of time.

Put 1 cup flour in a large mixing bowl. Bring the beer and ½ cup water to a boil. Immediately pour the liquid into the flour, and stir briefly and vigorously until the mixture is well blended and gruellike. Let cool to room temperature.

Dissolve the yeast in warm water. With your hands, stir together the yeast, beer mixture, and salt. Add enough of the flour so that you can turn the dough out onto a work surface. Knead and add remaining flour until the full amount is worked into the bread. You will encounter a good deal of stickiness along the way. Knead well for 10 minutes.

Shape the dough into a loaf approximately 14 inches long and 5 inches wide, and place on an oiled baking sheet. Cover with a towel and let the dough rise in a warm spot for around 1¼ hours.

Brush the loaf with egg yolk glaze, then, using a single-edged razor blade, make 5 shallow diagonal slashes along the top of the bread. Let rise for another 10 minutes. Preheat the oven to 350°F.

Bake the loaf for 45 minutes. It is done when it sounds hollow when rapped on the bottom with a fist. Let cool completely before cutting.

Salt-Rising Bread

Makes 2 loaves

If you make salt-rising bread the traditional way, with only a fermented cornmeal starter as a leavening, and make three different batches on three different days, you will most likely achieve three different results. The bread may or may not rise to a fully shaped loaf, depending on how powerfully the starter has fermented or on how ideal the fermenting conditions are. Though it is not traditional to add yeast, the small amount added in this recipe guarantees a risen loaf, and of course you will still have the salt-rising taste that makes this bread unique.

For the starter

1 cup milk
1 tablespoon sugar
½ cup cornmeal
1 teaspoon salt

1 teaspoon yeast
2 cups warm water
2 tablespoons sugar
3 tablespoons melted butter
Scant 8½ cups unbleached flour

Make the starter the night before you wish to bake bread. Scald the milk. Stir in sugar, cornmeal, and salt. Put the mixture in a mason jar and cover it with foil. Set the jar in a bowl. Run some hot tap water into the bowl until it comes halfway up the jar. Place bowl in a warm spot and let the cornmeal ferment overnight. In the morning there should be a settling of cornmeal, and a froth of bubbles on top of the liquid.

In a mixing bowl, dissolve the yeast in warm water. Add the starter. (So noxious do I find the odor of the fermented cornmeal—rather like a completely rotten potato—that I hold my nose during this step.) Add sugar, melted butter, and 2 cups flour and stir well. Cover and let rise in a warm spot for 45 minutes, at which point the mixture should be light and full of bubbles.

Add the remaining flour and knead the dough for 10 minutes. The dough should be rather firm. Divide dough in half, form each into a loaf, and place in buttered 9 x 5 x 3-inch loaf pans. Let rise until the dough rounds up nicely over the rims of the pans, 45 minutes or so.

Bake in a preheated 350°F oven for 1 hour.

Grandmother's Loaf with Crackled Crust

Makes 1 large loaf or 2 small loaves

This plump, bosomy loaf, flavored with a morsel of lard, brings comforting and evocative memories of a long-ago kitchen.

1 package yeast
1 cup warm water
1 cup warm milk
3 tablespoons unsalted butter
2 tablespoons lard
2 tablespoons sugar
2 teaspoons salt
About 4 cups all-purpose flour

For the crackled crust

3 tablespoons rice flour, toasted a medium brown in a frying pan
3 tablespoons cold water
3 teaspoons peanut oil

Dissolve the yeast in warm water. Stir in the warm milk.

Melt the butter and lard together. Stir in the sugar and salt, and when somewhat cooled, add to the yeast. Stir in around 3½ cups flour, or enough to make a solid dough. Turn the dough out onto a floured work surface and knead, continuing to add flour, for about 10 minutes. The dough should be medium-firm and nicely resilient to the touch. Put the dough in a greased bowl and let it rise in a warm spot until doubled in bulk.

Take the dough from the bowl, shape it nicely into a loaf, and place in a large oiled loaf pan. (Make 2 small loaves, if you wish.) Cover with a towel and let rise until the dough meets the top of the pan around the rim and the center of the loaf is about an inch higher than the rim.

Preheat the oven to 350°F.

Mix the crackled crust by stirring rice flour and cold water to a paste. Stir in the peanut oil. Brush the topping gently over the bread.

Bake for 1 hour.

The World's Largest Hamburger Bun

Makes 1 huge bun

1 package yeast	1½ teaspoons salt
¼ cup warm water	1 egg, lightly beaten
¼ cup milk	About 2½ cups all-purpose flour
½ cup evaporated milk	Heavy cream
4 tablespoons unsalted butter	Melted butter (flavored with
1 tablespoon sugar	garlic, if desired)

Dissolve yeast in warm water. Heat the milk and evaporated milk together until hot. Stir in butter, sugar, and salt, and let cool to luke-warm. Combine the yeast, milk mixture, and egg. Stir in around 2 cups of flour, then transfer the dough to a floured work surface and knead, adding the additional ½ cup or so of flour, until the dough is still quite soft but does not stick to your hands. Knead for about 10 minutes, or until the dough is elastic. Put the dough in an oiled bowl, cover, and let rise for 1 hour in a warm place.

Oil a rimless baking sheet (or turn over a rimmed one). Place the dough directly on the baking sheet and roll it out to a circle 13 to 14 inches in diameter. Try to keep the rim thinner and the center thicker. Let rise for 30 minutes.

Creating a huge hamburger is an amusing activity for a summer cookout or a children's birthday party. This mammoth bun will hold 2 to 3 pounds of meat cooked as one giant patty (cooked under the broiler, then reversed onto another dish to continue browning on the other side), a multitude of smaller patties, or lots of Sloppy Joe mixture.

Preheat the oven to 350°F. Just before baking, brush the surface of the loaf with cream. Bake for 40 to 45 minutes. If the crust feels at all crisp when the bun is taken from the oven, immediately transfer the bun to a counter and cover it with a towel to steam-soften the exterior. Let the bun cool, then split it, brush with lots of melted butter, and toast lightly before piling on hamburger.

Italian Picnic Loaf

1 large loaf, 8 generous servings
(Color plate 11)

This picnic loaf is a joy to look at and a pleasure to take along on an outing for lunch. The bread encases a full array of luncheon items, from eggs, cheese, and sausage to olives and red peppers.

1 package yeast
1⅔ cups warm water
2 teaspoons salt
About 4⅔ cups unbleached flour
1 4-ounce jar whole pimientos
1 pound provolone, Gruyère, or
   Muenster cheese
½ teaspoon lemon zest
1 large clove garlic, sliced

Small handful of parsley
1¼ pounds kielbasa sausage
8 eggs, at room temperature
¼ pound Niçoise olives

For the glaze
1 egg yolk beaten with 2
   teaspoons water

To make the bread base, dissolve the yeast in warm water. Add salt, then enough flour to make a mass that can be turned out onto a work surface. Knead, adding the remaining flour as necessary, until a firm dough results. Knead for 10 minutes, then put in an oiled bowl, cover, and let rise for 1 hour.

While the dough is rising, prepare the ingredients that the bread will hold. Drain the pimientos, and cut out 8 long 1-inch strips. Dice the remaining peppers, and blot all peppers as dry as possible. Cut the cheese into ½-inch cubes. Put lemon zest, garlic, and parsley together on a cutting surface. Mince them together until they are a fine and fragrant mash (there should be a good 2 tablespoons). Mix together the cheese, minced mixture, and diced peppers and set aside.

Cut the sausage into 4 pieces. Peel off the thin casing skin from the exterior of each piece.

When the dough has finished its rise, remove it from the bowl and pinch off one third of it and reserve. Roll out the large portion of dough to a circle 14 inches in diameter. Place the dough circle on an oiled baking or pizza sheet. Mound the cheese mixture in the center of the circle. Roll out two thirds of the reserved dough to a thin circle large enough to cover the cheese completely. Drape the dough over the cheese. Dip a finger into the egg yolk glaze and use the glaze to glue the bread together where it joins.

Place the 4 sausage sections around the exterior rim. Place 2 eggs between each sausage portion. Roll small strips of the remaining dough under your palms, then use them to secure the sausage and eggs to the bread base. Use more egg yolk glaze to attach the strips to the bread base.

Brush all exposed bread surfaces with egg yolk glaze. Arrange the 8 strips of pimiento radiating from the center of the bread over the cheese. Press most of the olives around the edge of the cheese dome and then arrange some in the center of the cheese (from which the peppers radiate).

Let the bread rise for 30 minutes. Bake in a preheated 375°F oven (the eggs will hard-cook in the process) for 30 minutes. Let the bread cool to room temperature.

Slicing between each pair of eggs, and again through the center of each sausage portion, divide the bread into 8 portions, with some of all the ingredients in each.

Take along a bottle of wine, and you will have a generous picnic lunch.

Swirled Red, White, and Green Bread

Makes 1 large loaf or 2 small loaves
(Color plate 13)

For the green dough
1¼ teaspoons yeast (½ package)
½ teaspoon sugar
¾ cup warm water
1 teaspoon salt
3 tablespoons spinach purée
  (cook spinach, squeeze dry,
  then press through a sieve with
  a pestle)
Generous 3 cups unbleached
  flour

For the red dough
1¼ teaspoons yeast
¼ teaspoon sugar

¾ cup warm water
1 teaspoon salt
4 tablespoons tomato paste
Scant 3 cups unbleached flour

For the white dough
1¼ teaspoons yeast
½ teaspoon sugar
1 cup warm water
1 teaspoon salt
About 3 cups unbleached flour

For the glaze
1 egg yolk beaten with 2
  teaspoons water

This bread is a handsome stripe of green, pale red, and white. Because it is composed in the patriotic colors of the Italian flag, it has always seemed to me particularly suitable with Italian meals. When the bread is sliced, spread with garlic butter, and lightly toasted, its flavors and colors intensify most pleasingly.

Use a separate bowl for each dough color. Put the yeast, sugar, and warm water in each of the three bowls. When the yeast has dissolved, add the salt. Add spinach purée to one bowl and tomato paste to another. Add flour to the spinach bowl first. Knead the dough firmly for 8 minutes, adding flour as necessary. The dough should not be sticky. Put in a bowl, cover with a towel, and set aside in a warm place to rise.

Add flour to the tomato mixture. Knead the dough for 8 minutes, then put in a bowl, cover with a towel, and set aside to rise.

Add flour to the white-dough bowl. Knead for 8 minutes. Set aside to rise in a covered bowl.

When the white bread has risen for 1 hour, start forming the loaf. First roll out the white dough to a rectangle 10 x 15½ inches. Nicely square up the corners. Roll out the red dough to the same size. Lay the red dough on top. Roll out the green dough, then lay the green dough on top of the red.

Roll the dough up the long way, like a jelly roll. You can now make 1 long loaf or, if you wish, cut the roll in half and bake 2 shorter loaves. Place the bread, seam down, on an oiled baking sheet. Gently pull the white dough down a bit over the coiled edges so that no red or green shows. Brush the top of the bread with egg yolk glaze.

Let the bread rise for 40 minutes. Bake in a preheated 350°F oven for 1 hour for a large loaf, 50 minutes for smaller loaves.

L'Artichaut (The Artichoke)

Makes 1 large loaf
(Color plate 14)

L'artichaut *was a popular bread form in eighteenth-century France. You could make it with all white dough, but try this two-tone, two-flavor loaf for interesting taste and texture.*

2 packages yeast
2¼ cups warm water
1 tablespoon salt
1 tablespoon sugar
¼ cup melted butter
About 5¾ cups unbleached flour
3 tablespoons molasses

1 tablespoon cocoa
2 cups whole-wheat flour

For the glaze
1 egg white beaten with 2
  teaspoons water

Dissolve the yeast in warm water. Add salt, sugar, melted butter, and 3¼ cups unbleached flour. Stir vigorously for 2 minutes. Divide the batter between two bowls.

To one bowl add molasses, cocoa, and whole-wheat flour. Turn the dough out onto a floured board and knead, adding a bit of unbleached flour if the dough seems at all sticky. Continue kneading for 10 minutes, until the dough feels firm and elastic. Place in an oiled bowl, cover, and let rise for 1 hour in a warm place.

To the second bowl add the remaining unbleached flour (around 2½ cups). Turn the dough out and knead it for about 10 minutes, until firm and pliable. Cover and let rise for 1 hour.

Take the white dough from the bowl and gently stretch it out as long as possible. Roll the dough out to a rectangle about 24 inches long and 5 or 6 inches wide. Roll out the whole-wheat dough to the same length and shape.

With a sharp knife, cut slits in each dough approximately 1½ inches apart and only 4 inches long so that the dough strips remain whole and uncut through their bottom 1½ to 2 inches—rather like a comb with fat prongs. Lay the whole-wheat dough on top of the white and roll up. Place on an oiled baking sheet with the pointed slits up. Gently spread and fan out the petals of the "artichoke." Round the petals at the tips and turn them this way and that until a pleasing pattern emerges. Cover with a towel and let rise for 45 minutes. Brush with glaze.

Preheat the oven to 350°F. Bake the bread for approximately 1 hour, or until it resounds with a hollow thump when knocked on the bottom.

The Cauliflower Loaf

Makes 1 large loaf
(Color plate 14)

This spectacular-looking loaf is surprisingly easy to form. The cauliflower adds a positive, almost grainy flavor to the dough. For artistic inspiration, study the shape of your cauliflower before you cook it.

For the dark dough

¾ cup warm water
1½ teaspoons sugar
1 package yeast
2 teaspoons molasses
2 tablespoons melted unsalted
    butter
1 teaspoon salt
1½ teaspoons cocoa
¾ cup whole-wheat flour
Generous 1¾ cups unbleached
    flour

For the light dough

1 package yeast
2 teaspoons sugar
¾ cup warm water
2 cups cooked, puréed
    cauliflower
2 tablespoons melted unsalted
    butter
1 teaspoon salt
About 5 cups unbleached flour

For the glaze

1 egg yolk beaten with 2
    teaspoons water

To make the dark dough, put warm water in a bowl. Add sugar, yeast, molasses, butter, and salt. Stir until dissolved. Add cocoa and flours. Turn the dough out onto a floured work surface and knead, adding flour, for 10 minutes, until the dough no longer feels sticky. Place in an oiled bowl, cover, and let rise for 1¼ hours.

Steam or boil the cauliflower until soft. Purée in a blender, food processor, or food mill.

To make the light dough, dissolve the yeast and sugar in warm water. Stir in the cauliflower purée, melted butter, and salt. Mix in flour until a dough that can be turned out of the bowl forms. Knead the dough on a floured work surface for 10 minutes. Add flour as necessary to form a fairly stiff dough. Place in an oiled bowl, cover, and let rise for 1 hour.

Roll out the dark dough to a rectangle approximately 25 inches long and 5 to 6 inches wide. Shape the length into a circle (there will be a hole in the center) on an oiled baking sheet. Wet the ends of the dough with water and press them together.

Remove the light dough from its bowl, twist off portions both large and small, and form them into balls. Put some unbleached flour on a plate and press one side of each ball into the flour. Arrange the balls, flour side up, on top of the dark dough in a rounded mound that resembles the white part of a cauliflower.

Tear off a long sheet of heavy aluminum foil. Fold it the long way into thirds and oil the top of the foil. Lift the dark dough up and fit the foil firmly around the outside of the dough. Tie a string around the foil, then fold the foil down slightly so that it forms a supporting ledge on which the dark dough can rest.

Snip the dark dough into 1½-inch-wide strips that resemble leaf-shaped sections, and arrange like the outer green portions of a cauliflower. Round some of the strips to suggest the cut portions of foliage surrounding the flower, then trim evenly with scissors. Brush the dark dough with egg yolk glaze. Let the bread rise for 45 minutes in a warm spot.

Preheat the oven to 350°F. Just before placing the bread in the oven, take a single-edge razor and make a multitude of small slits over the white dough to suggest the surface complexity of a real cauliflower. Sieve a little more unbleached flour over the bread to cover any bald spots. Bake for 1 hour, or until the bread sounds hollow when thumped on the bottom with a fist. Remove the foil, let cool, and serve.

White/Whole-Wheat/Rye Bread

Makes 1 large loaf
(Color plate 14)

2½ cups warm water
2 packages yeast
1 tablespoon sugar
1 tablespoon salt
4 tablespoons melted butter
About 4 cups unbleached flour
2 tablespoons molasses
1 teaspoon caraway seeds
1 tablespoon cocoa

1¼ cups rye flour
2 tablespoons honey
1¼ cups whole-wheat flour

For the glazes

I egg yolk beaten with 2
    teaspoons water
1 egg white beaten with 1
    tablespoon water

Put the warm water in a bowl and add the yeast and sugar. Let dissolve, then stir and add salt, melted butter, and 3 cups unbleached flour. Mix vigorously and well for a minute or two, then divide the batter evenly into three bowls.

Make rye dough first. Add molasses, caraway seeds, cocoa, and rye flour to one bowl. Turn the dough out and knead for about 8 minutes, until smooth and medium-firm. Put the dough in an oiled bowl; turn the dough in the bowl to oil the entire surface, then cover with a towel and let rise in a warm place.

To make whole-wheat dough, add honey to the second portion of dough. Stir well, then add whole-wheat flour until you can turn the dough out onto a floured work surface. Keep kneading and adding whole-wheat flour for about 8 minutes, or until the dough is medium-firm and not sticky. Put in an oiled bowl, turn the dough, cover, and set aside to rise.

To the third dough portion add the remaining 1 cup flour and turn the dough out. Knead, adding flour as necessary, until a firm dough develops. Put in an oiled bowl, cover, and set aside. Let the white dough rise for 1 hour; the other doughs will have a longer rising time.

At the end of the hour, lift the rye dough gently from its bowl. Pinch off a small portion (about the size of a large walnut) and reserve. Gently, so as not to deflate the dough any more than necessary, round the rye dough and place it on an oiled baking sheet. Take the whole-wheat dough, pinch off and reserve a walnut-sized portion, and form the remaining dough into a ball. Place it next to and barely touching the rye dough. Remove the white dough from its bowl and give it a brief knead to expel all air. Pinch off and reserve a small portion.

This very pretty three-flavored bread makes an excellent party loaf. The rye dough is always prepared first, as it is most sluggish in rising, then the whole-wheat, and finally the white. I like to serve this in a big basket with three accompanying cheeses —Brie or Camembert for the white bread, a nutty Appenzeller or Gruyère for the rye, and perhaps a cheddar for the whole-wheat portion.

Round the dough and place it by the other two breads to form a triangle.

Roll the reserved rye dough back and forth under your palms into a long rounded strand. Place the strand at the point where the rye and white loaves touch and coil it up the the center of the white loaf. (See color plate 14.) Round the reserved whole-wheat portion into a strand and curl it up from the whole-wheat–rye join to the center of the rye bread. Curl the white strand into the center of the whole-wheat loaf from the join of the white and whole-wheat. Cover the loaf lightly with a towel and let rise for 1 hour.

Brush the rye portion with egg yolk glaze. Brush the white and whole-wheat portions with egg white glaze. Bake the loaf in a pre-heated 350°F oven for 1 hour.

GRAIN BREADS

Here is bread, which strengthens man's heart,
and therefore called the staff of life.
Matthew Henry

Corn, wild rice, oats, granola, and wheat berries are only a few of the grains that lend their personalities to the healthy, hearty loaves in this chapter. My particular favorites are High-Protein Athletes' Bread, with 12 grams of protein per slice; my mother Betty's Whole-Wheat Buttermilk Loaves, which must be frozen before being eaten to develop their fine, aromatic crumb; and, perhaps most fun of all, Popcorn Bread, with 5 cups of popcorn kneaded in until they disappear in a plain white dough and its heightening butter-essence flavor—a delight both to make and to eat.

Popcorn Bread

Makes 1 loaf

1 package yeast
1¼ cups warm water
2 teaspoons salt
2 tablespoons unsalted butter,
  melted and browned

2 teaspoons butter-flavored
  extract
3½ cups unbleached flour
5 cups popped corn, coarsely
  crushed by hand

Five cups of popped corn and extra butter flavoring in a loaf of bread—what a surprise! And what a delicious loaf it creates. Try taking this bread to the movies.

47

Dissolve the yeast in warm water. Add salt, browned butter, and butter-flavored extract. Mix in 2 cups flour and stir well.

Add the popcorn and stir it into the soft dough; surprisingly, its bulk will almost disappear. Add in more flour until the dough can be turned out onto a work surface. Knead, adding flour, until a firm elastic dough has formed. Continue to knead for around 10 minutes.

Put the dough in a clean oiled bowl, cover, set in a warm place, and let rise for 1 hour, or until doubled in bulk. Butter a 9 x 5 x 3-inch loaf pan and gently place the bread in the pan. Let rise for another hour. Since this bread has a high fat content, it may be necessary to give the bread a little nudge by setting it to rise in a slightly warm oven.

Preheat the oven to 350°F. Bake the bread for 50 minutes. Serve with plenty of butter.

Wild Rice Bread

Makes 1 loaf

¾ cup wild rice
1 teaspoon salt
3 tablespoons vegetable oil
1 package yeast
1 cup warm water

1 tablespoon grated onion
¼ cup coarsely chopped shelled almonds
About 2½ cups unbleached flour

This is a delicious nutty, grainy, meaty loaf. It works well formed as a basket bread and is excellent served with a fashionable salad— say, of pungent arugula, radish cress, peeled walnut halves, and radicchio—all caressed with a garlic and nut oil dressing.

Put 1½ cups water in a saucepan. Add ½ cup wild rice and ¼ teaspoon salt. Bring to a boil and immediately reduce the heat to a simmer. Cook the wild rice for 15 minutes, then rinse and drain. Grind it in a food processor or blender until well chopped. It should be mealy rather than mushy. Set aside.

Heat the oil in a deep wide pot. Add 2 tablespoons raw wild rice and pop it as you would pop corn. Keep an eye on it as it pops so it does not overbrown. Keep a lid over the pot, leaving it a bit ajar so steam can escape. Shake the pan or stir the rice frequently. Some grains will turn white like long thin popcorn; the rest will simply expand and lighten in texture and color. The volume will double in around 3 minutes. Remove the wild rice with a slotted spoon. Pop the final 2 tablespoons wild rice in the oil remaining in the pan. Set the popped wild rice aside. Discard the oil.

Dissolve the yeast in warm water. Add the onion, cooked wild rice, remaining ¾ teaspoon salt, almonds, and 2 cups flour. Turn the dough out onto a floured work surface and knead briefly. Knead in the popped wild rice and additional flour as needed to make a smooth, workable dough. Knead vigorously for 8 minutes.

Put the dough in a lightly oiled bowl, cover, and let rise in a warm spot for 1 hour, or until doubled in bulk.

Form the dough in either a large loaf pan or in a basket. (See "On Basket Breads," page 13.) Let rise for 1 hour, or until doubled in bulk. It will need a fairly long rising time, due to its dense texture.

Bake the bread in a preheated 325°F oven for about 1 hour, or until the loaf sounds hollow when thumped on the bottom with a fist.

Yeasted Scottish Oat Baps

Makes 1 loaf with 4 divisions

1 cup plus 2 tablespoons rolled oats	1 egg, separated
3 teaspoons salt	1 cup oat flour
3 tablespoons brown sugar	¾ cup Scotch or Irish steel-cut oatmeal
1½ envelopes yeast	About 3 cups unbleached flour
¼ cup warm water	

Bring 2 cups water to a boil. Stir in 1 cup rolled oats, salt, and brown sugar and set aside to cool to lukewarm.

Dissolve the yeast in ¼ cup warm water. In a large bowl, stir together the cooked oatmeal, yeast, egg yolk, oat flour, and steel-cut oats. Continue adding unbleached flour until a dough emerges that is firm enough to turn out of the bowl. Knead, adding flour as necessary, to make an unsticky but still moderately soft dough. Knead for 10 minutes, then put the dough in an oiled bowl, cover with a towel, and set aside to rise for 1 hour, or until doubled in bulk.

Remove the dough from the bowl and divide it into 4 portions with a knife. Shape each portion into a round. Place the rounds not quite touching each other on an oiled baking sheet, to create a four-leaf-clover shape. Cover with a towel and let rise for 40 minutes, at which point the breads will have grown into a whole unit. Preheat the oven to 350°F.

Beat the egg white with 1 tablespoon water, then gently brush it over the baps. Sprinkle the remaining 2 tablespoons rolled oats over the bread.

Put the bread in the oven and immediately lower the heat to 325°F. Bake for 45 to 50 minutes. Remove from the oven. Put the bread on a cooling rack and cover the top with a towel for 10 minutes to lightly soften the upper crust.

This is a good crusty, grainy loaf that makes an excellent accompaniment to hearty soups or stews. If oat flour is too difficult to find, unbleached flour may be substituted.

Sticky, Crusty Corn Bread

Makes 12 to 15 servings

The thinner this corn bread is made, the better it seems to be. For a handsome presentation, heat an oiled skillet, spoon on corn bread batter in an open flower petal design, and let the flower fry to a golden brown. Pour the rest of the batter into a baking pan, place the design on top, and finish baking in the oven.

4 tablespoons unsalted butter, softened	1 tablespoon granulated sugar
½ cup all-purpose flour	1 tablespoon baking powder
1 cup yellow cornmeal, preferably stone-ground	1 teaspoon salt
	1 egg, beaten
1 tablespoon brown sugar	1¼ cups buttermilk
	3 tablespoons melted shortening

Use the 4 tablespoons of butter to generously grease the bottom and sides of a 10-inch round iron baking pan, or a standard 9 x 13-inch or 11 x 15-inch baking pan. Set the pan in the oven. Preheat the oven to 400°F.

Mix the flour, cornmeal, sugars, baking powder, and salt in a mixing bowl. Make a well in the center of the dry ingredients and add the egg, buttermilk, and melted shortening. Stir until the batter is just blended.

Pour batter into the baking pan (by now the butter should be sizzling and slightly browned). Smooth the batter as neatly and rapidly as possible. Set the pan on the lowest rack of the oven and bake for about 25 minutes (slightly less for larger pans). Test by cutting out a small bottom portion of the cornbread. The bottom should be a dark, crunchy, caramelized golden brown.

Scottish Oat Cakes

Makes 15 oatcakes

These rustic cakes are a traditional Scottish specialty, and they taste just like the expensive imported oatcakes found in specialty food shops. They are good with cheese.

2 teaspoons lard	2 tablespoons heavy cream or buttermilk
2 teaspoons unsalted butter	¼ teaspoon salt or ½ teaspoon sugar
½ teaspoon sugar	
¼ teaspoon salt	
2 cups coarse steel-cut oatmeal	
1 scant cup flour, preferably oat flour, but all-purpose will also do	

Heat ¾ cup water in a saucepan. Put the lard, butter, sugar, and salt in a mixing bowl, and when the water comes to a boil, pour it over the ingredients. Stir briefly, then add oatmeal and continue to stir until everything is well mixed and the oats begin to become slightly sticky.

Sprinkle some flour over the oats and work the mass together with your hands. Keep adding flour, but only the minimum amount to bind the oats together so that they can be turned out and kneaded. The less flour the better.

Knead the oat dough briefly, then press it down on a lightly floured surface and roll it out as thin as possible. Cut out 3-inch rounds and transfer them to a buttered baking sheet. Continue rolling and cutting oatcakes until all the dough is used. Using the bottom of a glass tumbler, press down on the rounds to flatten any portions that look overly thick.

Let the cakes sit while the oven preheats to 325°F. Just before putting the cakes to bake, brush them with cream or buttermilk flavored with either ¼ teaspoon salt or ½ teaspoon sugar, depending on whether you prefer a slightly salty or slightly sweet finish. Bake for 12 to 15 minutes. If baked correctly, the cakes should not color, although they should be completely dry. Cover with foil if necessary. Let cool and store in an airtight container.

Boston Brown Bread

Makes 1 loaf

¼ teaspoon ginger
½ cup cornmeal
½ cup rye flour
½ cup whole-wheat flour
1 teaspoon baking soda

½ teaspoon salt
⅓ cup molasses
1 egg, lightly beaten
¾ cup buttermilk

A *traditional American steamed bread, long appreciated by lovers of molasses.*

Butter a 1½-quart mold. Traditionally, you would use a cylinder, such as a large coffee can, but you might choose a charlotte or soufflé mold.

Combine the ginger, cornmeal, rye and wheat flours, baking soda, and salt in a bowl and mix well. Make a well in the center and add the molasses, egg, and buttermilk in two or three portions. Stir until well blended.

Spoon the batter into the greased mold and tap the mold on a counter to settle the contents. Cut wax or parchment paper, drape it over the top of the mold, and tie string around the paper to hold it in place. (This keeps steam from dripping back onto the bread.)

Place a small cake rack (I use a metal cookie-cutter ring) on the bottom of a large pot that has a cover. Set the mold on the rack. Bring some water to a boil in a separate pan or kettle and pour it down the side of the pot until it comes halfway up the mold. Cover the large pot and adjust the heat to maintain a perfect steaming effect. (There should be no shimmering on the water's surface, no turmoil to cause the mold to rattle.)

Steam for 3½ hours, adding more water as necessary to maintain the proper level.

Preheat the oven to 325°F. Remove the mold from the water and cut away the paper cover. Put the mold in the oven for 20 minutes to dry the bread. Let cool briefly, then unmold.

Cracked Wheat Kernel Bread

Makes 1 large loaf or 2 small loaves

I *find the wheaty complexity of this loaf very appealing, for wheat puffed and boiled and raw all go into its making.*

3 tablespoons vegetable oil
1 cup whole-wheat berries (hard red winter wheat grains)
¾ cup bulgur (cracked wheat)
2 packages yeast

1½ cups warm water
2 teaspoons salt
½ cup gluten flour
About 4½ cups unbleached flour

Put the oil in a large pan with a lid. Heat it, and when hot, add ⅓ cup wheat berries. Cover the pot and shake it over the heat, exactly as if you were making popcorn. The wheat will pop in the pan. (It will not look like popcorn, but each grain will double in size. Do not let it burn.) These kernels are now crunchy and splendid-tasting. Set them aside and discard the oil.

Bring 1½ cups water to a boil in a saucepan. Add the remaining ⅔ cup wheat berries and let them cook at a rolling boil for about 4 minutes, or until they are just chewable. (Test after 3 minutes.) Add the bulgur to the pan and cook for another 30 seconds. Remove from the heat and drain wheat into a sieve.

Dissolve the yeast in warm water. Add the salt, boiled bulgur-wheat mixture, and gluten flour. Stir in 2 cups unbleached flour, then the popped wheat berries. Continue adding flour until the dough can be turned out onto a work surface. Knead, adding flour as necessary, until a firm, elastic dough results. Knead for 8 minutes.

Put in a clean oiled bowl, cover with a towel, and let rise in a warm spot for 1 hour.

Form into 1 large round on a baking pan, or 2 small loaves in buttered loaf pans. A basket could also be used. (See "On Basket Breads," page 13.) Let the loaves rise again until doubled in bulk.

Bake in a preheated oven set halfway between 325° and 350°F. Bake for 50 to 55 minutes for a large loaf, 45 minutes for small loaves. The bread is done when the bottom sounds hollow when rapped with a fist.

Sprouted Wheat Berry Bread

Makes 1 loaf

1 package yeast
1 tablespoon brown sugar
1¼ cups warm water
¼ cup toasted wheat germ

2½ teaspoons salt
½ cup whole-wheat flour
1 cup sprouted wheat berries
About 2¼ cups unbleached flour

Dissolve the yeast and brown sugar in warm water. Stir in the wheat germ, salt, whole-wheat flour, and wheat berries. Add enough unbleached flour so that the dough can be turned out on a work surface. Knead, adding more flour as necessary, until the dough is no longer sticky. Knead for 10 minutes. The dough should be medium stiff, as it tends to soften during its rise. Put the dough in an oiled bowl, cover with a towel, and let rise for 1 hour.

Punch the dough down, knead slightly, and form into a loaf. Place in an oiled 9 x 5 x 3-inch loaf pan and let it rise in a warm spot for another hour, or until it has nicely doubled in bulk and risen to the top of the pan.

Bake in a preheated oven halfway between 325° and 350°F. Bake for 50 to 60 minutes, or until the loaf sounds hollow when knocked on the bottom with a fist.

Note: Here is what you do: Take a 1-pint mason jar and cut a small round of plastic or metal screen or even nylon mesh to fit the top. Put ¼ cup wheat kernels (hard red winter wheat is what is usually available in shops) in the bottom of the jar. Fill the jar with water, then place the screen over the top, fasten on the lid, and set the jar in a dark place overnight. The next morning, drain the water completely, rinse and drain the sprouts, and set the jar in a dark place. That evening, rinse and drain again. Repeat the watering-draining process morning and night for 4 or 5 days, or until the jar grows full of sprouts.

This is a wonderful, chewy bread, and you must not be deterred from making it by the idea of cultivating sprouting wheat.

Granola Loaf

Makes 1 loaf

1½ packages yeast
1 tablespoon honey
1½ cups warm water
¾ pound (3 cups) granola (such
   as Familia)

¼ cup raisins
½ teaspoon salt
About 3¼ cups unbleached flour

A crisp, grainy loaf with all the flavor and goodness of granola to enhance it.

In a large bowl, add the yeast and honey to warm water and let them dissolve.

Put the granola in the bowl of a food processor fitted with a steel blade and pulse the machine on and off about five times to break up and half grind the granola. Add the granola, raisins, and salt to the yeast. Stir in flour until a dough results that can be turned out onto a floured surface. Knead and add flour until the dough is still soft but no longer sticky. Continue kneading for 10 minutes, then put the dough in an oiled bowl, cover it, and let rise for 1 hour.

Shape the dough into a free-form loaf on an oiled baking sheet. Let rise for 30 minutes.

Bake in a preheated 350°F oven for 45 to 50 minutes, or until the loaf sounds hollow when you knock its bottom with a fist. Place a damp towel over the bread as it cools, to soften the top crust.

High-Protein Athletes' Bread

Makes 1 dense loaf

2 packages yeast
2 cups warm water
2 egg whites
1 tablespoon poppy seeds
2½ teaspoons salt
¼ cup nonfat dry milk

¼ cup wheat germ
2 cups gluten flour
⅔ cup soy flour
½ cup whole-wheat flour
About ¾ cup unbleached flour

This is an athletes' bread that contains a complete protein. Technically, this bread with butter on it could sustain one for a considerable period of time. Cut the bread into 16 slices and each will contain 12 grams of protein. Two slices and you have close to the equivalent protein of a cheeseburger.

Dissolve the yeast in warm water. Mix in the egg whites until well blended. Add poppy seeds, salt, dry milk, wheat germ, gluten flour, and soy flour. Stir well. Add the whole-wheat flour and enough of the unbleached flour to allow the dough to be turned out onto a work surface. Knead the bread, adding more flour as necessary, until a medium-firm, unsticky dough emerges. Knead for 10 minutes.

Put the dough in a clean oiled bowl. Cover with a towel and let rise until doubled in volume, 1 generous hour. Form the dough into a loaf. Put it in a buttered 9 x 5 x 3-inch loaf pan and let rise until the dough billows over the top of the pan.

Bake in a preheated 350°F oven for 45 to 50 minutes, or until the loaf sounds hollow when knocked on the bottom with a fist.

Betty's Whole-Wheat Buttermilk Loaves

Makes 2 loaves

¾ cup sugar
2 tablespoons unsalted butter, softened
2 tablespoons shortening
1 egg

2½ teaspoons baking soda
2¼ cups buttermilk
1 cup all-purpose flour
2¾ cups whole-wheat flour

This is a peculiar bread in that it must be frozen before it is eaten. The freezing process moistens the crumb and intensifies the flavor of these succulent loaves.

Preheat the oven to 350°F. Butter two loaf pans.

Cream together the sugar, softened butter, and shortening. Stir in the egg and blend well. Dissolve the baking soda in buttermilk and add to the batter. Stir in the flours in two or three additions, and mix until just blended.

Divide batter between the pans. This bread tends to overly rise in the center, so spoon the batter up and toward the sides of the pans. Bake for 50 to 60 minutes. Test the bread by inserting a skewer. It should come out perfectly dry.

Remove breads from the oven, cover with a towel, and let cool for 5 minutes before turning them out of the pans. Let cool, then foil wrap the breads and season in the freezer at least overnight. Thaw the loaves and serve at room temperature.

Seeded Whole-Wheat Bread

Nourishing and full of seeded subtlety, this whole-wheat bread is a family favorite.

Makes 1 large loaf or 2 small loaves

3½ packages yeast
3 tablespoons honey
1 tablespoon light molasses
2 cups warm water
3 tablespoons melted unsalted
  butter
2 teaspoons salt

Large pinch ginger
1 tablespoon sesame seeds
1 tablespoon poppy seeds
½ cup wheat germ
2½ cups whole-wheat flour
Generous 2¾ cups unbleached
  flour

Dissolve the yeast, honey, and molasses in warm water. Mix in melted butter, salt, ginger, seeds, and wheat germ. Add the whole-wheat flour and enough white flour to form a dough that can be turned out of the bowl. Knead, adding flour as necessary, until the dough is smooth and no longer sticks to the palm of the hand. Knead for a good 10 minutes. Put the dough in a clean oiled bowl, cover with a towel, and let rise in a warm place for 1 hour.

Remove the dough from the bowl and shape it into 1 large round or 2 small loaves to fit loaf pans. Let the bread rise again for a good hour . . . it is a sluggish dough.

Bake in a preheated oven set halfway between 325° and 350°F. Bake for 50 minutes for a large loaf, 40 minutes for small loaves, or until the bread sounds hollow when tapped on the bottom with a fist.

Light Rye Round

This is a light rye— light in spirit, texture, and flavor—and it makes a handsome rustic-looking loaf.

Makes 1 large or 2 small rounds

2 packages yeast
2 tablespoons honey
1½ cups warm water
1½ tablespoons salt (yes)
3 tablespoons melted butter
3 eggs (reserve 1 yolk)
1 tablespoon caraway seeds
2 cups rye flour
2 cups whole-wheat flour
2 cups unbleached flour

For the topping

1 tablespoon rye flour
1 tablespoon unbleached flour
1 tablespoon bran

For the glaze

1 egg yolk (reserved) beaten with
  2 teaspoons water

In a large bowl, dissolve the yeast and honey in warm water. Add salt and melted butter. Lightly beat the eggs (minus 1 yolk) and add to the liquid. Stir in caraway seeds, rye flour, whole-wheat flour, and enough unbleached flour to form a dough that can be turned out of the bowl. Knead the dough on a floured work surface, adding unbleached flour as necessary, until a dough of medium-firm consistency results. Knead well for 10 minutes, then put the dough in an oiled bowl, cover with a towel, and let rise in a warm spot for 1½ hours.

Turn out the dough and form into 1 or 2 rounds. Place the bread on an oiled baking sheet. To make the topping, mix rye flour, unbleached flour, and bran in a cup. Add just enough water (about 3½ tablespoons) to make the mixture the consistency of thin wallpaper paste—just loose enough so it will heavily drip down the sides. Let the bread rise for 30 minutes, then brush with the egg yolk glaze.

Spread the topping on the bread and let the paste flow irregularly toward the sides. Take a single-edged razor blade and cut 5 radial slashes wheel-spoke fashion from the center of the bread. Let rise, uncovered, for another 20 mintues. Preheat the oven to 350°F.

Bake the rye round 1 hour for a large loaf, 45 to 50 minutes for smaller rounds, or until the loaf sounds firm and hollow when tapped on the bottom.

Medium Rye Bread

Makes 1 large loaf or 2 small loaves

3 to 4 slices firm bread, preferably crusts of rye or whole-wheat
3 envelopes yeast
2¼ cups warm water
3 tablespoons melted unsalted butter
1 ounce unsweetened chocolate, melted

½ cup molasses
1 tablespoon salt
½ teaspoon ginger
2 teaspoons instant coffee
2 tablespoons caraway seeds
2 cups rye flour
1 cup whole-wheat flour
2¼ cups unbleached flour

This is a moist, particularly succulent rye bread with a sweet, crisp crust. The browned crumbs—an old European trick for fostering flavor and economically using up the crust of last week's loaf—add a toasty quality to the bread.

Toast the bread until very dark and grind it to fine crumbs in a food processor or blender. Set aside.

In a large bowl, dissolve the yeast in warm water. Stir in melted butter and chocolate, molasses, salt, ginger, coffee, and caraway seeds and mix well. Add 1 tablespoon caraway seeds, rye flour and whole-wheat flours, the toasted crumbs, and enough unbleached flour to form a kneadable dough. Turn the dough out onto a work surface and continue kneading, adding flour as necessary to make it of medium consistency—not so soft that it sticks to the hands, but not so hard as to present kneading difficulties. Continue kneading for 10 to 12 minutes. Put the dough in an oiled bowl, cover with a towel, and let rise in a warm spot for 1½ hours.

Gently remove dough from the bowl and form it into 1 large round or 2 small rounds. (This bread is also nice formed in a round or oblong basket heavily floured with rye flour.) Let the bread rise for another 50 to 60 minutes. Ten minutes before baking, you can, if you wish, apply Rye Paste for a bakers' finish. (See page 16.) With a razor blade, cut 5 short lines radiating from a center point on the top of the loaf. Preheat the oven to 350°F. Bake for 1 hour for a large loaf, 50 minutes for small loaves.

Miche

Makes 1 large loaf
(Color plate 12)

*M*iche *is a large, flat rye loaf that is made in many areas of provincial France. To arrive at its crisscrossed dark and light surface, the loaf must be formed in a basket. This bread is an excellent accompaniment to cheeses and a handsome addition to a display of various breads.*

1 package plus 1 teaspoon yeast	3 tablespoons bran
2 cups warm water	1 cup whole-wheat flour
2 tablespoons sugar	1½ cups rye flour
1½ teaspoons salt	About 2½ cups unbleached flour
¼ cup bulgur wheat (couscous)	

In a large bowl, dissolve the yeast in warm water. Add the sugar, salt, bulgur, bran, and whole-wheat and rye flours. Mix well. Add the unbleached flour and mix, using one hand to hold the bowl and the other to half knead, half mix the dough, until very soft dough is formed. Turn the dough out onto a lightly floured work surface. Knead and work the dough for 10 minutes, stretching, pulling, and slapping it as vigorously as possible. Put the dough in an oiled bowl, cover with a towel, and let rise for 1 hour.

Prepare a basket (see "On Basket Breads," page 13), or simply lay towels in a basket at least 12 inches in diameter and sieve a ¼-inch layer of flour over the bottom. Roll out the dough to a thickness of 1 inch and lay it in the basket. Cover the basket with a towel and let rise for 30 minutes. Uncover.

Put an oiled baking pan on top of the basket, then turn pan and basket over together, so that the dough unmolds onto the pan. With a single-edge razor, make slits about 2 inches apart across the dough in one direction, then crosshatch it, making a diamond pattern. Cover with a towel and let the dough rise for another 20 minutes. Preheat the oven to 350°F.

Bake the *miche* for approximately 40 to 45 minutes. The bread should sound firm when you knock a fist on the bottom. Put the bread down on a flat surface and cover with a towel to steam the crust a bit. Remove the towel after 15 minutes, stand the bread on edge, and gently knock it on a surface to remove any excess flour.

Variation A handsome Italian loaf, dubbed "the pocketbook," can also be shaped from this dough. On an oiled baking sheet, pat and shape the dough into a long triangle with rounded points. Using your fingers, divide the dough at the top point so that a circle or "handle" forms at the top of the loaf. Cover and let rise for 30 to 40 minutes. Bake the loaf in a 350°F oven for 40 to 45 minutes.

One frequently sees this "pocketbook" bread hung on the arms of shoppers in parts of southern Italy.

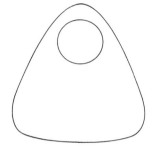

Dark Moist Russian Bread

Makes 1 loaf

1 cup finely ground crumbs from firm rye bread
1½ packages dry yeast
¼ cup blackstrap molasses
3 tablespoons unsalted butter
⅓ cup sugar
2 teaspoons instant coffee

3½ tablespoons sieved cocoa
¼ teaspoon orange zest
1 tablespoon poppy seeds
1 teaspoon ginger
½ cup gluten flour
About 3½ cups rye flour

This bread is enhanced by the dark toasted flavor of rye bread crumbs. The Russian procedure is to save the crusts from the loaf previously made, then crush them and add them to the next batch of bread, so that each loaf in turn carries on the spirit and the essence of its predecessor.

Put the rye bread crumbs in a flat pan and slide under a heated broiler. Shaking the pan frequently, toast the crumbs until they are a deep brown. Set aside.

Dissolve the yeast in ⅓ cup warm water. Bring 1⅓ cups water to a boil in a saucepan. Remove from the heat and add molasses, butter, sugar, and instant coffee. Stir until the molasses is dissolved. Let the mixture cool to barely warm, then add it to the yeast.

Add cocoa, orange zest, poppy seeds, ginger, gluten flour, and 2 cups rye flour to the yeast. Stir well, then add the toasted bread crumbs and enough of the remaining rye flour so that the dough can be turned out onto a work surface. Knead the dough well for at least 10 minutes, adding flour as necessary. The dough tends to stickiness, so you should continually flour the work surface and work the dough until the flat of your palm, pressed into the center of the dough mass, comes out clean. Put the dough in an oiled bowl, cover with a towel, and let rise in a warm spot for 1 hour. You will not see a great deal of expansion.

Form the dough into a round on an oiled baking sheet. Cover again with a light towel and let rise in a warm spot for around 1½ hours.

Bake in a preheated oven set halfway between 325° and 350°F. Bake for around 50 minutes, or until the heavy loaf sounds hollow when tapped on the bottom with a fist.

LITTLE BREADS, MUFFINS, AND ROLLS

Coffee and rolls,
Barbarous rolls;
Sing coffee,
Black coffee,
Vile coffee and rolls!
    A. P. Herbert

Here is an assortment of little breads—Raspberry Muffins, Buttermilk Cushions, Angel Biscuits, and Singing Hinneys. You will find rolls (soft, medium, and hard), Wheaty Breadsticks (shaped like stalks of wheat, to mass in a centerpiece basket), and a spectacular round of Swiss Potato Rolls.

If you have heretofore had trouble producing professional-quality bagels, popovers, or English muffins, try the new techniques and recipe formulations presented here and see if you are not happily surprised with the results.

Peanut Butter Muffins

These crunchy peanut butter muffins will especially be enjoyed by children.

Makes 16 muffins

1¾ cups all-purpose flour
2 teaspoons baking powder
½ teaspoon salt
¼ cup sugar
⅓ cup peanut butter, preferably crunchy style

1 cup milk
2 eggs
½ cup chopped peanuts (roasted, skinless, with excess salt shaken off)

Preheat the oven to 350°F. Butter 16 muffin cups.

In a mixing bowl, stir together the flour, baking powder, salt, and sugar.

61

In another bowl, mix the peanut butter and milk, stirring in the milk bit by bit until the peanut butter is diluted and smooth. Stir in the eggs and half the peanuts.

Stir the liquid mixture into the dry ingredients all at once. Stir only until the batter is moderately blended and still somewhat lumpy.

Spoon the batter into the muffin cups, filling them only two thirds full. Quickly sprinkle the remaining peanuts over the top.

Bake for 25 to 30 minutes. Turn out and let cool before serving.

Sour Cream and Bran Muffins

Makes 16 muffins

The secret of good light muffins is not to overbeat them. Another good trick is to leave 2 or 3 cups empty in each muffin pan; after filling the pan with muffin batter, fill the empty spaces with a bit of hot water, which will steam during cooking and keep the muffins moist.

1½ cups all-purpose flour
½ cup bran
1 teaspoon baking powder
2 tablespoons sugar
½ teaspoon baking soda

½ cup coarsely chopped walnuts
1 cup sour cream
1 egg, lightly beaten
2 tablespoons molasses

Preheat the oven to 350°F. Butter 16 muffin cups.

In a mixing bowl, mix together the flour, bran, baking powder, sugar, baking soda, and nuts.

In another bowl, stir together the sour cream, egg, and molasses.

Add the sour cream mixture to the dry ingredients all at once. Stir quickly and just to the point where the ingredients are mixed; they will still be somewhat lumpy.

Fill the muffin cups two thirds full. Pour hot water into any empty cups.

Bake for 25 minutes. Turn the muffins out and serve warm. These are also good lightly toasted.

Cornmeal Custard Cups

Makes 20 to 24 muffins

These tender, eggy little muffins are delicious served hot with very cold butter.

2 cups milk
2 tablespoons unsalted butter
¾ cup cornmeal

1 teaspoon salt
3 eggs

Preheat the oven to 400°F. Butter 24 muffin cups.

Put the milk and butter in a pan and bring to a scald. Immediately remove from the heat.

Mix cornmeal and salt in a mixing bowl. Make a well in the center and gradually beat in the milk with a whisk until all lumps disappear. Add the eggs, one at a time, whisking after each until well blended. Put the muffin tins in the oven to heat briefly.

Pour the batter into the muffin tins, filling each cup half full. Bake for 30 to 35 minutes if you are using heavy iron pans, 25 to 30 minutes if you are using lighter aluminum pans. To test for doneness, insert a skewer in the center of a muffin; it should come out clean. Do not overbake. Serve hot.

Leftover Bread Crumb Muffins

Makes 12 muffins

1 cup fine dry bread crumbs, lightly toasted
1 tablespoon unsalted butter
1½ tablespoons sugar
1 teaspoon salt
½ cup milk, just at a boil
½ cup cold milk
1 egg, lightly beaten
1 teaspoon seeds (see NOTE)
3 teaspoons baking powder
¾ cup all-purpose flour

Preheat the oven to 375°F. Grease 12 muffin cups.

Place the crumbs, butter, sugar, and salt in a bowl. Pour the hot milk over the ingredients, mix them all together, then set aside to cool for 5 minutes.

Stir in the cold milk, then the egg and 1 teaspoon seeds of choice.

Mix baking powder and flour together. Stir quickly into the batter, beating rapidly and briefly.

Spoon the batter into the muffin cups. Top each muffin with a light sprinkling of seeds.

Bake for 25 minutes. Serve warm.

Note: On seeds: If the crumbs are rye, use caraway seeds; if the crumbs are whole-wheat, use poppy seeds; if the crumbs are white or corn, use sesame seeds.

It was a toss-up as to whether to put these muffins in the uses-for-leftover-bread chapter or in the muffin section. Any kind of dry leftover bread can be used in this recipe—rye, corn bread, whole-wheat, or white—so that at whim you can turn these muffins into rye muffins, corn mufins, whole-wheat muffins, or whatever. This is an old, very frugal recipe—one your ancestors would be proud of you for using.

Raspberry Muffins

Makes 16 muffins

For the topping
3 tablespoons light brown sugar
½ teaspoon cinnamon
1½ tablespoons butter, chilled

For the muffins
1½ cups all-purpose flour
2 teaspoons baking powder
½ teaspoon salt

½ cup sugar
2 teaspoons baking soda
1 egg, lightly beaten
¾ cup buttermilk, at room
   temperature
1 tablespoon melted butter
10 ounces frozen raspberries,
   thawed

For the topping, mix the brown sugar and cinnamon and set aside. Cut the chilled butter in 16 thin shavings and set aside.

Preheat the oven to 400°F. Butter 16 muffin cups.

In a mixing bowl, stir together the flour, baking powder, salt, sugar, and baking soda.

In another bowl, stir together the egg, buttermilk, melted butter, and raspberries, including the juice.

Stir the liquid ingredients into the dry. Mix until the batter is combined—barely 15 seconds or so—the batter will be slightly lumpy.

Fill the muffin cups two thirds full. Rapidly sprinkle some topping mixture over each muffin and dot each with a piece of butter.

Bake for 25 minutes. Serve warm.

Bacon Biscuits

Makes 12 biscuits

These biscuits are quickly made and taste delicious with scrambled eggs. I much prefer them to traditional Southern ham biscuits.

3 strips lean bacon
2 cups all-purpose flour
2 teaspoons baking powder
½ teaspoon baking soda
1 teaspoon salt

1 tablespoon unsalted butter,
   softened
⅔ cup buttermilk
Melted butter or buttermilk for
   brushing tops

Preheat the oven to 450°F.

Fry the bacon until crisp. Pour off 1 tablespoon of the rendered fat as the bacon fries and reserve it. Crumble the bacon.

In a bowl, mix together the flour, baking powder, baking soda, and salt. Sprinkle the reserved bacon fat over the flour and add the butter.

Using your fingers, rub in the fat until it disappears into the dry ingredients. Add the bacon and buttermilk and stir until the dough is soft and light but not sticky. Turn dough out onto a floured board.

With floured hands, knead the dough just until smooth. Do not overwork.

Roll dough out to a ¾-inch thickness and cut out biscuits with a 3-inch round biscuit cutter. Place the biscuits on an ungreased baking sheet.

Bake for 12 to 15 minutes, at which point the biscuits should have a golden brown top crust. Remove from the oven and immediately brush tops with melted butter or buttermilk.

Serve warm.

Singing Hinneys

Makes 1 bread divided into 4 portions, 8 to 10 servings

4 cups all-purpose flour
2 teaspoons salt
5 teaspoons baking powder
1 tablespoon vegetable shortening
   or lard

2 cups less 2 tablespoons milk, slightly warmed

Mix the flour, salt, and baking powder together in a bowl. Rub in the shortening or lard until it completely disappears. Make a well in the center and stir in the milk to make a moderately stiff dough.

Put the dough on a floured surface, flatten it down neatly with your hands, and cut into 4 portions. Shape each portion into a ball, then flatten each ball with the palm of your hand.

Arrange the dough portions so they just touch each other (in a square pattern) on a greased hot griddle set on a low burner or in an electric skillet set at 325°F. Cook for approximately 25 minutes, or until the bread is golden brown on the bottom. Gently turn the entire bread over and continue cooking for another 20 minutes, until brown on the other side.

Split the Hinneys open and load them with unsalted butter. To serve, reassemble the Hinneys and cut into wedges. Serve jam on the side.

Singing Hinneys— what a delightful name—are simple breakfast or tea breads from the British Isles. They are rather like overgrown Southern-style biscuits, and they are meant to be split, buttered, and jammed. The "singing" consists of mild spits and hisses during cooking. I tell you this so you will not be disappointed when arias fail to float from your skillet.

Sweet Potato Biscuits

Makes about 15 large biscuits or 24 small biscuits

These spicy yellow plantation-style biscuits can be made from either sweet potato or pumpkin.

2 cups all-purpose flour
2 teaspoons baking powder
1¼ teaspoons baking soda
1 teaspoon salt
½ teaspoon cinnamon
½ teaspoon ginger

2 tablespoons unsalted butter, cut into bits
¾ cup sweet potato or pumpkin purée
About ½ cup buttermilk
3 tablespoons melted butter

Preheat the oven to 400°F.

In a bowl, mix together the flour, baking powder, baking soda, salt, cinnamon, and ginger. Add the butter and work it into the flour with your fingertips until it disappears.

Make a well in the center of the dry ingredients and add the sweet potato purée and half the buttermilk. Stir together, adding the remaining buttermilk in 2 more portions, until the dough is soft and light. Do not overbeat.

Turn the dough out onto a floured board and knead briefly (20 to 30 strokes) until the dough is smooth. Roll the dough out to a thickness of ¾ inch. Cut out biscuits with a 2- or 3-inch cutter and place them on ungreased baking sheets.

Bake for 12 to 15 minutes, or until the tops are speckled with gold. Take from the oven and immediately brush the tops with melted butter. Serve hot.

Buttermilk Cushions

Makes 2 dozen rolls

Serve these soft, delicate creatures fresh, hot, and dripping with butter.

1 package yeast
¼ cup warm water
4 tablespoons melted butter
¼ teaspoon baking soda
1 cup buttermilk
2 eggs, lightly beaten

¼ cup sugar
4½ cups sifted all-purpose flour

For the glaze
1 teaspoon honey mixed with 1½ tablespoons melted butter

Dissolve the yeast in warm water. Stir in melted butter.

In a mixing bowl, dissolve the baking soda in buttermilk. Add the yeast. Stir in eggs, sugar, and 1 cup flour and stir vigorously for 1 minute. Add the remaining flour and knead until the dough is very smooth. Put it in an oiled bowl and let rise for about 1 hour, or until doubled in bulk.

On a lightly floured surface, roll out the dough into a rectangle until it is ½ inch thick. Cut the dough into 1½-inch squares. Place on greased baking sheets and brush with honey-butter glaze. Let rise in a warm place for 20 to 30 minutes. Preheat the oven to 375°F.

Bake for 12 minutes. Serve with extra honey-butter for dipping.

Angel Biscuits

Makes 30 to 40 biscuits, depending on cutter size

1 package yeast
¼ cup warm water
¼ cup vegetable shortening
¼ cup unsalted butter
5 cups all-purpose flour

1 tablespoon baking powder
2½ teaspoons salt
⅓ cup sugar
2 cups buttermilk

Dissolve the yeast in warm water. Melt the vegetable shortening and butter together and let cool until warm but no longer hot.

Mix the flour, baking powder, salt, and sugar in a bowl. Make a well in the center and add yeast, melted fat, and buttermilk. Grasp the handle of a heavy spoon and stir firmly. The dough will be quite sticky. After the dough is well beaten, cover the bowl with a towel and let rise for 1½ hours.

Stir the dough down and beat it vigorously. Cover and refrigerate for at least 3 to 4 hours. (The dough will keep for a week.)

When ready to bake, spoon out a portion of dough and roll it out on a floured board to a thickness of ⅜ inch. Use a 2- or 3-inch round cutter to form the biscuits. Place the biscuits on a buttered baking sheet and brush the tops with melted butter. Let rise in a warm spot for 20 to 30 minutes.

Bake in a preheated 400°F oven for 15 to 20 minutes, or until the biscuits are wonderfully browned.

This recipe hits halfway between biscuits and rolls, in that it is shaped and cut like biscuits but leavened like both rolls and biscuits. These biscuits are made in many places in the South, where warm breads frequently appear at breakfast along with grits or ham and red-eye gravy. The dough keeps for 6 or 7 days in the refrigerator, so portions can be twisted off and baked into fluffy breads for an entire week.

Quick Batter Rolls

Makes 24 rolls

These rolls can be rapidly executed. (Fresh rolls in 1¼ hours if you move right along!) They have crisp, buttery exteriors. The dough can be stirred by hand, but if you have a mixer, let it do the work for you.

1½ cups hot water
⅓ cup (5⅛ tablespoons) unsalted butter
3 tablespoons sugar
2 envelopes yeast

1½ teaspoons salt
1 egg, lightly beaten
4 cups sifted all-purpose flour

Put 1½ cups hot tap water in mixing bowl. Add butter and sugar. When the butter has melted, add the yeast, salt, and egg. Add 2½ cups flour and beat for 2 minutes on the machine (or by hand). Add the remaining flour and mix for another 2 minutes.

Cover the bowl with plastic wrap and let the dough rise in a warm place for 30 minutes.

Butter 24 muffin cups.

Stir the batter down with 20 strokes. Drop the batter into the tins. Set in a warm place and let rise for 20 minutes.

Preheat the oven to 400°F. Bake the rolls for 12 to 15 minutes, until nicely browned. Serve warm.

Classic Dinner Rolls (Soft Puffy Rolls)

Makes 24 rolls

This is the perfect recipe for making Parker House, cloverleaf, or any other variety of small, soft dinner rolls. It was used by Mrs. Margaret Latta, who sold delicious rolls for more than forty-five years at the Women's Market in Chapel Hill, North Carolina. This is a relatively small amount of dough.

1 package yeast
¼ cup sugar
1 cup warm water
1½ teaspoons salt
1 tablespoon melted vegetable shortening

1 tablespoon melted butter
1 egg
1½ cups flour

Dissolve the yeast and sugar in warm water. Add salt, the melted shortening and butter, and the egg. Stir well, then add the flour and beat until well blended. Turn the dough out onto a work surface and knead for only 3 or 4 minutes. The dough should feel very smooth.

Put dough in a greased bowl and turn it over in the bowl to grease its top side. Cover with a damp tea towel and let rise in a warm spot for about 1 hour, or until doubled in bulk.

Parker House Rolls After the first rising, roll out the dough on a floured surface to a thickness of ⅜ inch. Cut 3-inch circles with a biscuit cutter. Brush the tops of the rounds with melted butter. Fold rounds over into halves and place them, not quite touching, on a greased baking sheet. Let rise until nearly doubled in bulk, then bake in a preheated 350°F oven for about 15 minutes, or until lightly browned.

Take from the oven and brush tops with melted butter. Slide the rolls onto a counter. For very soft rolls, cover the top with a kitchen towel as the rolls cool.

Cloverleaf Rolls After the first rising, pinch off small bits of dough and shape them into rounds the size of a small walnut. Butter muffin tins and place 3 balls of dough in each cup. Let rise until nearly double in size. Bake in a preheated 350°F oven for 15 minutes, or until lightly browned. Brush the tops with melted butter and turn the rolls out of the tins.

Shaped Rolls (Medium-Firm Rolls)

Makes 18 rolls

2 packages yeast
1 teaspoon sugar
¼ cup warm water
¾ cup warm milk
1½ teaspoons salt
1 egg, lightly beaten
About 3 cups of flour

For the glaze
1 egg yolk beaten with 1
   tablespoon water

For the topping
Seeds, such as poppy, sesame,
   etc. (optional)

Here is a recipe for good, flexible dough that fits perfectly between soft Parker House-type rolls and crisp, hard club rolls. Use this dough for all sorts of shaped rolls —kaiser rolls, knots and spirals, small braided rolls, etc.

Dissolve the yeast and sugar in warm water. Stir in the milk, salt, and egg. Add half the flour and stir well. Continue adding flour until the dough can be turned out of the bowl onto a work surface. Knead vigorously for 10 minutes, adding flour as necessary, until a very smooth, pliable, yet relatively firm dough results. The dough should not feel at all sticky.

Oil a bowl, put the dough in the bowl, and turn the dough so all its surface is coated. Cover the bowl with a damp towel and place in a warm spot for 1 hour.

Cut off portions of dough and form them as desired into rolls. (This recipe makes 18 rolls of decent size.) Place them on an oiled baking sheet and let rise until doubled in bulk. (Keep a pot of water steaming nearby during this rising to help the top crust stay tender.) Brush with egg yolk glaze and sprinkle with seeds, if you wish.

Preheat the oven to 425°F. Put a pan of hot water on the lowest oven rack. Bake the rolls for 12 to 15 minutes.

Club Rolls

Makes 12 rolls

This simple roll recipe divides nicely into crisp, hard rolls.

1 package yeast
1 tablespoon sugar
1¼ cups warm water
1 teaspoon salt
2 tablespoons melted unsalted
　butter
1 egg white, beaten to a foam
1 tablespoon lightly toasted flour

About 4⅓ cups all-purpose flour
Cornmeal

For the glaze
1 egg yolk beaten with 2
　teaspoons water and a pinch
　each salt and sugar

Dissolve the yeast and sugar in warm water. Add salt, melted butter, and egg white. Add toasted flour, stir, and then add 3 cups all-purpose flour and mix well. Turn the dough out onto a floured work surface and knead for about 8 minutes. Continue to add flour until a moderately firm dough is formed. Put the dough in an oiled bowl, cover with a damp towel, and let rise in a warm spot for 1 hour.

Scatter cornmeal lightly on a work surface. Turn the dough out and gently pat it into a 10 x 14-inch rectangle. Square up the edges and sides as evenly as possible. Divide the dough in half lengthwise with a knife. Cut 5 vertical lines through the dough to divide it into 12 rolls. Place the rolls on an oiled baking sheet and square them up neatly. Let them rise for 20 minutes, or until the rolls look almost fully formed. Brush them with the egg yolk glaze.

Bake in a preheated 350°F oven for 25 minutes.

Wheaty Breadsticks

Makes 15 breadsticks
(Color plate 17)

Mass these in a basket for a pretty presentation of individual wheat-shaped bread sticks. The addition of cornmeal to the dough makes the crust crisp and tasty.

⅓ cup yellow cornmeal
1½ packages yeast
1½ cups warm water
¼ teaspoon sugar
2 tablespoons rye flour
2 teaspoons salt

About 4¾ to 5 cups unbleached
　flour

For the glaze
1 egg yolk beaten with 2
　teaspoons water

Put 1 cup water in a small pan and bring to a boil. Stir in cornmeal. Remove from the heat and let cool to warm.

Dissolve the yeast in warm water. Stir in the sugar, rye flour, salt, and cornmeal. Add unbleached flour and mix the dough until it can be turned out of the bowl onto a floured work surface. Continue to knead in flour until the dough is firm, with no hint of stickiness. Put in an oiled bowl, cover, and let rise in a warm place for 1 hour.

Oil two large baking sheets. Divide the dough into 15 portions. Using your hands, roll out each portion, creating a "stem" 8 to 10 inches long. Leave a thick portion of dough at one end, flatten it slightly, and shape into a long head of wheat. Place the sticks on the baking sheets.

When all the wheat stalks are formed, brush them with egg yolk glaze. Using scissors, cut a dividing line down the center of each head (do not cut through to the baking tray). Snip 4 rows of wheat kernels along the head. Let sticks rise for 10 minutes.

Preheat the oven to 350°F. Bake the breadsticks for 10 minutes. At the end of this time, they should be firm on the bottom. Turn each stick over so it can brown on the top and bake for another 10 to 12 minutes, at which time the sticks should be golden brown but not too hard. Mass upright in a basket and serve fresh.

Whole-Wheat *Ballons*

Makes 20 rolls

1½ packages yeast
1 teaspoon sugar
1½ cups warm water
1 cup warm milk
2 tablespoons melted unsalted
    butter
3 teaspoons salt
3 cups whole-wheat flour
About 2½ cups unbleached flour

For the glaze
1 egg white beaten with 1
    teaspoon water

For the topping
Your choice of ⅓ cup bran,
    oatmeal, or caraway seeds

These plump, round crusty rolls have such a mild whole-wheat flavor that they can be used for any dinner party.

Dissolve the yeast and sugar in warm water. Stir in the milk, melted butter, and salt. Add the whole-wheat flour and stir well, then start adding unbleached flour until a soft dough forms. Turn the dough out onto a floured surface and knead for about 10 minutes, adding flour as necessary, until dough no longer feels sticky and is firm and elastic.

Put it in an oiled bowl and turn to coat the entire surface. Cover with a towel and let stand in a warm place for about 1½ hours, or until doubled in bulk.

Oil a baking sheet. Remove the dough from the bowl and divide into 20 portions. Form each portion into a ball and place on the baking sheet. Brush lightly with egg white glaze, then sprinkle with bran, caraway, or oatmeal. Cover loosely with a towel and place in a warm spot for 45 minutes. Preheat the oven to 400°F.

Just before baking, using a single-edged razor blade, make a light slit through only the very top surface of each ball. Bake for 20 to 25 minutes. Let cool on racks.

Swiss Potato Rolls in a Basket

Makes 32 rolls
(Color plate 12)

This recipe makes a delicious, puffy round of break-apart rolls that are very good for entertaining. I give you here a large amount of dough that makes 32 rolls. These rolls are formed in a basket 16 inches in diameter, then turned out on a 16-inch pizza pan to bake. If you wish, you can easily halve this recipe, forming the rolls in a 12-inch basket for a yield of 16. You might make two smaller rounds from the larger recipe and freeze one.

1½ cups potatoes (about 3 medium), peeled and cut into cubes
2 teaspoons salt
4 tablespoons unsalted butter, cut into pieces

1 tablespoon sugar
2 packages yeast
11 cups all-purpose flour, or as needed

Put the potatoes and salt in a saucepan with 2 cups water and bring to a boil. Lower the heat and cover. Cook for 12 to 15 minutes, until the potatoes are tender enough to purée.

Remove the pan from the heat and drain, reserving the potato cooking water. Press potatoes through a sieve with the back of a large spoon. Stir butter and sugar into the potatoes.

Measure the potato water and add enough cold water to bring the amount to 3 cups. Heat; when the liquid is just warm, dissolve the yeast in the potato water. Add to the potatoes.

Stir in 8 cups flour, then continue adding flour and kneading until the dough can be turned out of the bowl. Knead for 10 minutes, adding flour as necessary to make a smooth and elastic dough.

Put the dough in a clean oiled bowl, cover with a towel, and let rise for 1 hour, or until doubled in bulk.

If you do not have a lined basket, prepare one by fitting one or two clean kitchen towels into the basket. Sieve a ¼-inch layer of flour over the bottom of the basket. (See "On Basket Breads," page 13.) Oil a 16-inch pizza pan.

Turn the dough out onto the floured surface. Divide it in half, then into quarters, then, using a dough scraper or metal spatula, separate into 32 pieces and form them into balls. Place 4 balls as a square in the middle of the basket, then place the other balls around them in a circular fashion. The gaps between them will fill in as the dough rises. Cover and let rest in a warm spot for 45 minutes.

Preheat the oven to 350°F.

Uncover the basket. Put the pizza pan, oiled side down, over the basket. Invert, remove the basket, and lift off the bottom towels. Let the dough rise for another 15 minutes.

Bake for around 40 minutes, or until nicely golden. Remove from the oven and either slide the roll cluster onto a wire rack or tilt it slightly to release steam from the bottom. Cover with a towel to soften the upper crust. Serve warm.

Note: If you wish, a hot iron rod can be used on the white surface to mark divisions between the rolls. (See scorched design, page 16.)

Frying Pan Crumpet Cakes

Makes 5 or 6 crumpet cakes

2 cups flour
1 teaspoon salt
1 envelope yeast
½ cup warm water
1 cup milk, slightly warmed

½ teaspoon baking soda
¼ cup lukewarm water
4 to 5 tablespoons butter for
    frying

You don't have crumpet rings? Never mind; this frying pan version makes delicious large golden breads that can be cut into halves or quarters, as you wish.

Put the flour and salt in a metal mixing bowl and set the bowl over low heat. Stir until the flour is slightly warm to the touch. (Flour can also be heated in a pan in a low oven, then removed to a mixing bowl.)

Dissolve the yeast in warm water. Make a well in the center of flour, add the yeast, and stir. Using a mixer equipped with a dough hook, beat for a full 5 minutes. Cover the bowl with a towel and let rise in a warm place for 1 hour.

At the end of the hour, dissolve the baking soda in lukewarm water. Add to the batter and beat by hand or machine for 2 minutes. Cover and let rise for 30 to 45 minutes more, or until you can see a light, slightly bubbled texture on the surface of the batter.

Melt 1 tablespoon butter in a 9- or 10-inch frying pan. Spoon in a portion of the batter and immediately smooth it as best you can over the bottom of the pan and up to the sides. Do not make the cakes too thick, and remove any excessive batter immediately. Let the crumpet cake fry over medium-low heat for about 5 minutes, or until the bottom is speckled and golden. Turn the crumpet cake with a spatula (or flip it over if you are adept), and let it cook for another 5 minutes. Two frying pans may be kept busy if you wish to speed up the process. Keep frying until all cakes are made.

Serve warm, with plenty of butter. These make good tea offerings, and they can be splendid at breakfast when topped with runny fried or poached eggs.

Bagels

Makes 12 bagels

1½ tablespoons liquid malt extract
1 package yeast
2 teaspoons salt
½ cup gluten flour
2 cups Pillsbury's Bread Flour
Cornmeal

For the glaze
1 whole egg beaten with 1½ tablespoons water and ¼ teaspoon salt

For the topping
Coarse salt or poppy seeds (optional)

If you try to make bagels from most recipes, you are likely to be doomed to disappointment. A passable roll-like object will emerge, but not one with the dense, chewy dough that pulls so nicely against the teeth, or the thick, almost-crisp crust that is so pleasurable to bite into. I am indebted to baker Sheldon Glick for all the information necessary to turn out the following near-professional product. The gluten flour is a necessity. As there are several fast-moving steps toward the end of production, read this recipe carefully before acting on it.

Run tap water as hot as it will go. Measure ½ cup very hot water, add the malt extract, and let it dissolve. Measure ½ cup warm water, add the yeast, and let it dissolve. Combine the two liquids in a mixing bowl.

Stir in salt, gluten flour, and 1 cup bread flour. Beat vigorously. Add the remaining flour and turn the dough out onto a board. Knead hard and thoroughly for 10 to 12 minutes. You must make a strong effort here to develop the gluten.

When the dough is elastic, divide it immediately into 12 portions. To form bagels, either roll each portion back and forth under your palms until it forms a cylinder 10 inches long and then join the ends to form a circle; or make a ball from each portion, stick two fingers through its center from both sides, and twirl the dough larger and larger until it forms a bagel shape. In any case, each bagel should be 4 inches across with a 2½-inch hole in the center. Scatter a light covering of cornmeal on a baking sheet and place each bagel on the tray as you form it. Let the bagels rise for about 20 to 25 minutes, until they are full and puffy-looking.

Ten minutes before the bagels finish their rise, coordinate the following:

1. Dust another baking sheet with cornmeal.

2. Bring a large pot of water to a full boil. Regulate to a good simmer.

3. Put a large heavy baking sheet in the oven. Preheat the oven to 500°F.

4. Preheat the broiler unit.

Gently place a bagel in the water. It should stay on the surface. (If it sinks, count the seconds it takes to float; for each second, give the bagels 1 more minute to rise.) Add another bagel or two to the pot, but do not crowd. Remove each bagel after 30 seconds and place it on the baking sheet dusted with cornmeal. Continue poaching the bagels.

When all the bagels are on the baking sheet, immediately place the sheet under the broiler for about 1 minute, at which point the bagels should be firm, lightly crusted, and golden brown on top. Watch them closely.

Immediately take them from under the broiler, brush the tops with egg yolk glaze, and sprinkle with salt or poppy seeds, if you wish. Shove the bagels off the baking sheet and onto the hot sheet in the oven. Bake for 8 minutes.

Note: If the broiler is not separate from the oven, preheat the oven first, then turn up to broil the bagels, then reduce the temperature. As soon as the broiler is no longer hot, bake the bagels in the oven.

English Fork-Apart Muffins

Makes sixteen 3-inch muffins

1⅔ cups milk	1 egg
2½ tablespoons unsalted butter	2 teaspoons salt
1 package yeast	1 tablespoon vinegar
1 heaping tablespoon sugar	5 cups unbleached flour
⅓ cup warm water	Cornmeal
1 tablespoon barley malt extract (optional)	Vegetable oil for frying pan

Heat the milk and butter together until butter melts. Set aside to cool.

Dissolve yeast and sugar in warm water. Add barley malt extract at this point if you wish.

Combine the milk mixture, yeast mixture, egg, salt, vinegar, and half the flour. Using a mixer or by hand, beat for about 3 minutes, until dough is smooth and well developed. Add the remaining flour

I am very fond of this English muffin recipe. The top and bottom crusts are firm, the center is spongy and receptive to butter, and the muffins fork apart easily. The vinegar not only adds piquancy to the taste, but also acts as a preservative.

and continue to mix for about 6 minutes, until the dough no longer clings to the sides of the bowl. Cover the bowl with plastic wrap and let rise in a warm spot for 1 hour.

Sprinkle cornmeal into a bowl. Using a large spoon and your hands, lift out a ½-cup portion of the dough and place it in the cornmeal. Turn the dough over in the meal, then lift it out and place on a baking sheet. Flatten it into a rough circle around 3 inches in diameter. Continue to make muffin shapes. Let them rise for around 8 minutes, then transfer them in batches to a hot very lightly oiled or nonstick frying pan. Cook over medium-low heat for about 6 minutes on each side. The muffins should be lightly browned on both sides and still slightly spongy when pressed in the center.

Crunchy Cheddar Biscuits

Makes twelve 4-inch biscuits

½ cup butter, softened
1 cup grated cheddar cheese
1 teaspoon salt
½ teaspoon Tabasco sauce

½ teaspoon Worcestershire sauce
1 cup all-purpose flour
1 cup unsweetened puffed rice
  cereal

This biscuit is very "short" and flaky—a biscuit in the English sense. Make it with a sharp or extra-sharp commerical cheddar or more expensive Canadian or New York cheddar—the biscuit is good with any of them. Serve as an hors d'oeuvre, as an accompaniment at a wine tasting, or simply as one of many crackers with fruit and cheese.

Preheat the oven to 325°F.

Put the butter, cheese, salt, Tabasco and Worcester sauces in a bowl and mix well. Sprinkle on the flour and, using your fingers, work everything together, just as you would a piecrust, until a smooth cohesive dough results.

Slowly add the rice cereal, working the dough until all the cereal bits are absorbed and scattered throughout. Divide the dough into 12 portions and place them on an oiled baking sheet. Flatten each portion until it is as round and thin as possible, then take a fork and press the dough, leaving tine marks all over the surface. Neaten the rounded edges, creating circles 4 inches in diameter.

Bake biscuits for 12 to 15 minutes, or until light brown. Let cool and store in an airtight container.

Poppy Seed Popovers

Makes 12 popovers

2 eggs
1 cup milk, quite warm
1 tablespoon melted butter

½ teaspoon salt
1 cup all-purpose flour
1 tablespoon poppy seeds

This is a standard recipe for popovers, except for the poppy seeds. The seeds will float to the top and form a tasty crust.

Preheat the oven to 425°F. Butter a popover pan generously. Put the pan in the oven just as you begin to beat the batter ingredients.

Put the eggs, milk, melted butter, salt, flour, and half the poppy seeds in a mixer or blender. Beat or blend for 3 minutes.

Take the hot pan from the oven and pour in the batter. Fill each cup half full. The pan should be so hot that it hisses when the batter touches it. Sprinkle the batter with the remaining poppy seeds and place immediately in the oven. Bake for 15 minutes. Reduce the heat to 350°F and continue baking for 15 minutes more.

Turn out from the pan immediately and place in a napkin-lined basket. Serve at once.

Note: Popovers, which are a kind of Yorkshire pudding in a cup, can be troublesome to make. If your oven heats unevenly, one corner of a batch may rise heroically while another sags in concave despair at the other side of the pan. Without the correct helpful thrust of bottom heat to generate steam and push the batter upward, the entire product can sit sullen and unmoving in its cups (in which case you announce, "We're having egg muffins for breakfast," for they will still taste good).

To make perfect popovers, it seems to me the following steps are necessary:

1. Use a real popover pan (heavy cast iron); grease and heat it before adding batter.

2. Beat the batter thoroughly.

3. Bake the popovers first at high heat, then reduce to medium heat.

4. No oven peeping during popping.

ESSENCE BREADS AND THEIR BUTTERS

The expert bread maker tends to smugness.
So intense is the satisfaction with the
product that it promotes self-satisfaction.
If you don't believe this, watch the expression
on a woman's face when she announces,
"It's home made."

Dorothy Thompson

This chapter contains a variety of breads based overwhelmingly on one clear, pure ingredient. Pumpkin, pears, chocolate, nuts, mushrooms, olives, mustard, and cheese—each lends its presence indisputably, so that every loaf has a distinctive "soul," a flavor heightened to its greatest intensity. With many of these breads, you will be asked to prick a network of holes over the surface and then to pour over the warm loaf a complementary syrup or juice that permeates with additional fragrance. Also, each recipe suggests a jam or butter that further develops the theme.

For new taste experiences, try Mustard Bread with its golden freckle of surface seeds, or Chocolate Chip Bread with its own Chocolate Nut Butter. Delight guests with Baked Potato Breads, each shaped like an oversized potato and crusted with crisp "skin," which are split and topped with melting butter, sour cream, and a greening of chives.

Most of these breads make satisfying presents.

Olive Bread with Tapenado

Makes 1 loaf
(Color plate 18)

A flavorful, Provençal-inspired bread to serve with its own container of that rustic olive spread, Tapenado, and a salad of rough and wild greens.

1 package yeast
1½ cups warm water
4 anchovy fillets
1 large garlic clove, peeled
1¼ teaspoons salt
2 tablespoons olive oil
½ cup black Niçoise olives, pitted and finely chopped
¼ cup jumbo pitted black olives, finely chopped
Generous 4¼ cups unbleached flour

For the glaze
1 egg yolk beaten with 2 teaspoons water

For the topping
8 anchovy fillets
8 jumbo pitted black olives
Coarse salt
Olive oil

In a mixing bowl, dissolve the yeast in warm water. Mash the anchovy fillets and garlic to a purée in a small mortar, or simply chop them and mash with the side of a knife. Add purée to the yeast. Stir in salt, olive oil, and both types of chopped olives. Add enough flour to form a cohesive dough, then turn the dough out onto a floured board and continue to knead for 10 minutes, adding flour until the dough is no longer sticky. Oil a bowl with olive oil and put the dough in it. Cover with a towel and let rise in a warm spot for 1 hour.

Remove dough from the bowl, form it into a ball, and place it on an oiled baking sheet. Press the center of the dough down with a 4-inch soufflé dish or tamp down a 4-inch circle with a mug until the dough resembles a doughnut with a thin web of dough across its hole. (If you have a soufflé dish of the correct size, you can actually bake it right in the bread.) Brush the bread with the egg yolk glaze. Make X's with the anchovy fillets at four points around the rim of the bread. Cut the olives in half and press a half at each intersection of the anchovies. Scatter a small handful of coarse salt around the rim of the bread, and drizzle a bit of olive oil over the top, particularly over the anchovy and olive decorations.

Let rise for 40 minutes, then bake in a preheated 350°F oven for about 50 minutes. The bread should sound hollow when tapped on the bottom. Let the loaf cool, then fit a soufflé dish or a small rustic bowl in the bread's center hollow and fill the dish with Niçoise olives or with Tapenado.

Tapenado

1 small garlic clove, mashed or
   minced
½ cup Niçoise olives, pitted
6 anchovy fillets (or to taste),
   minced

1 teaspoon lemon juice
A few capers
Salt and pepper to taste
Olive oil

Put the garlic, olives, and anchovy fillets in a blender or food processor and blend briefly until everything is very finely minced. Stir in the lemon juice, capers, and salt and pepper. Stir in just enough olive oil so that the mixture is of a spreading consistency, much like peanut butter.

Rosemary Focaccia with Rosemary Garlic Butter

Makes 1 flat bread

1 tablespoon rosemary leaves,
   fresh or dried
1 package yeast
1 teaspoon salt
1 tablespoon powdered rosemary

¼ cup olive oil
About 2⅓ cups unbleached flour
1 egg yolk
1 teaspoon coarse sea salt

Bring 1¼ cups water to a boil. Pour it over the fresh or dried rosemary leaves, then crush the leaves with a pestle to release the flavor into the water. Let the water cool to warm, then strain out the rosemary and reserve it. Add the yeast to the flavored water.

When the yeast has dissolved, add salt, the powdered rosemary, and 1 tablespoon olive oil. Stir in flour until the dough can be turned out of the bowl onto a kneading surface. Knead the dough well for 10 minutes, adding more flour as necessary, until a smooth soft dough results. The dough should be just beyond sticky in its handling point —add the minimum of flour. Put in a bowl oiled with 1 tablespoon olive oil. Turn the dough in the bowl so all sides are oiled. Cover with a towel and set in a warm spot to rise for 1 hour.

Grease a large baking sheet with olive oil. Remove dough from the bowl as carefully as possible and place on the baking sheet. Pat and stretch the dough out to a rectangle roughly 10 x 12 inches. Using the

This large flat Italian bread, with its small pockets of rosemary, oil, and salt, is one of the tastiest herb breads I know. Serve it with red meat stews, hot or cold lamb of any sort, rustic salads and, of course, with its own fragrant butter. It is best topped with fresh rosemary leaves. If powdered rosemary is not available, pulverize dry leaves in a mortar.

flat of your thumb, press a series of indentations all over the top of the bread, approximately 2 inches apart. Beat the egg yolk with 1 tablespoon olive oil and 1 teaspoon water and brush over the bread. Sprinkle the reserved rosemary over the surface. Drizzle surface with the last tablespoon of olive oil. Sprinkle on the coarse salt. Let rise for 45 minutes.

Bake in a preheated 350°F oven for around 25 minutes. Let cool and serve fresh with Rosemary Garlic Butter.

Rosemary Garlic Butter

8 tablespoons (1 stick) unsalted butter, softened
¼ small garlic clove, pressed

½ teaspoon powdered rosemary
Large pinch salt

Cream together butter, garlic, rosemary, and salt. Mound onto a serving dish and top with a sprig of fresh rosemary.

Sage Stuffing Bread

Makes 1 large loaf

If you like good old-fashioned sage stuffing as much as I do, you will adore this bread, which has all the elements of stuffing in it.

1 large onion, chopped fine
1 tablespoon unsalted butter
½ cup plus 2 tablespoons chicken stock
½ pound mushrooms, cleaned, trimmed, and chopped
1½ packages yeast
½ cup warm water

2 teaspoons celery seed
1 tablespoon dried rubbed sage
1½ teaspoons salt
2 tablespoons finely chopped parsley
½ cup gluten flour
About 3¾ cups unbleached white flour

Put the onion, butter, and 2 tablespoons chicken stock in a frying pan. Cover and cook over low heat until the onion is tender, about 12 minutes. Add the chopped mushrooms, turn up the heat, and sauté the mushrooms briefly, stirring constantly, until all liquid has disappeared from the pan and the mushrooms are dry and squeaky against the pan's surface. Set aside to cool.

In a large bowl, dissolve the yeast in warm water. Add the remaining ½ cup chicken stock. Stir in the celery seed, sage, salt, parsley, and gluten flour. Stir in the mushroom-onion mixture.

Add unbleached flour until a dough results that can be turned out onto a kneading surface. Knead, adding flour as necessary, until a firm dough results. Knead for another 8 minutes. The dough should be stiff now, as it softens and loosens during its rising period. Put the dough in an oiled bowl, cover, and set in a warm place to rise for 1 hour, or until doubled in bulk.

Form the dough in a 9 x 5 x 3-inch loaf pan, or in a basket (See "On Basket Breads," page 13). Let the bread rise for a good 45 minutes, or until it is well up over the edge of the pan. (If using a basket, turn the bread out onto a baking pan and let rise again briefly.)

Bake in a preheated 350°F oven for 50 to 60 minutes, or until the loaf sounds hollow when thumped on the bottom.

Three Greens Bread with Green Herbed Butter

Makes 1 very green loaf

1 cup grated unpeeled zucchini
   (1 large zucchini)
1½ teaspoons salt
½ pound fresh spinach,
   stemmed, or 10 ounces frozen
   spinach, cooked and squeezed
   as dry as possible
⅓ packed cup chopped scallions
8 tablespoons (1 stick) melted
   butter

½ cup vegetable oil
2 eggs, lightly beaten
2 tablespoons sugar
1 teaspoon baking powder
1 teaspoon baking soda
¼ cup buttermilk
3 cups unbleached flour

A beautiful green bread tasting thoroughly of vegetables, this loaf is not to be confused with that frequently simpering creature known as Zucchini Bread. Enjoy this bread spread with ricotta cream cheese flavored with mild herbs, or Green Herbed Butter.

Let the grated zucchini sit for 5 minutes, then take it up by handfuls and squeeze it through a sieve placed over a bowl. Measure the rendered juice and keep squeezing until you have ¼ cup liquid. Reserve the liquid. Sprinkle the zucchini with ½ teaspoon salt and set aside while you prepare the other vegetables.

Butter a large loaf pan. Preheat the oven to 325°F.

Put the spinach, scallions, and reserved zucchini liquid in a blender or food processor and purée. Reserve 1 teaspoon for the Green Herbed Butter. Put the remaining purée in a large bowl and add 1 teaspoon salt, melted butter, vegetable oil, eggs, and sugar. Stir well.

Take up the salted zucchini and again squeeze it by handfuls until it is as dry as possible. Add it to the purée mixture. Add the baking powder.

Sprinkle the baking soda over the buttermilk and add to batter. Stir in the flour in three additions and mix evenly, making sure that no clumps of white dough remain.

Scrape the dough into the loaf pan. Bake for about 1 hour. At the end of the hour, test with a wooden skewer. If it comes out with wet batter, continue baking for an additional 5 minutes or so.

Let the bread cool completely before cutting, as it is rather tender.

Green Herbed Butter

1 teaspoon spinach-scallion purée
8 tablespoons (1 stick) unsalted butter, softened
1 teaspoon finely minced parsley
½ teaspoon minced chives or ¼ teaspoon very finely minced scallion white
Pinch sugar

Put all ingredients in a bowl and cream together until smooth and well blended. I like to heap this on a pretty savoy cabbage leaf for presentation.

Sweet Red Pepper Bread

This bread is spectacular-looking, and one of the tastiest loaves in this book. Serve it for lunch with Italian sausage and a delicious dessert.

Makes 1 loaf
(Color plate 21)

2 medium-large onions
2 large garlic cloves, thinly sliced
4 tablespoons olive oil
3 large sweet red peppers, seeded
1½ packages yeast
1 cup warm water
1 tablespoon sugar
2 teaspoons salt
⅛ teaspoon cayenne pepper
⅛ teaspoon powdered saffron (optional)
Freshly ground pepper
About 4 cups unbleached flour
1 egg, lightly beaten
¼ teaspoon finely minced fresh or dried oregano

Chop 1 onion. In a covered frying pan, cook the onion and garlic in 2 tablespoons olive oil over low heat until very tender. Chop 1 red pepper and add to the pan. Continue cooking until the pepper is fork-tender and limp. Purée the onion-pepper mixture in a blender or food processor and set aside. Cut another pepper into fine dice.

In a large bowl, dissolve the yeast in warm water. Add the sugar, salt, cayenne, saffron, several grinds of fresh pepper, onion-pepper purée, and diced raw pepper. Add 3 cups flour, or enough to form a soft dough that can be turned out onto a floured surface. Knead for 10 minutes, adding flour until the dough is firm. Place in an oiled bowl, cover with a towel, and let rise in a warm spot for 1 hour.

While the bread rises, cut the remaining onion into slices ½ inch thick. Separate the rings and cook them in the remaining 2 tablespoons olive oil over low heat until almost tender. Cut the remaining red pepper into strips. Add to the onion and cook until tender. Let cool.

Take the dough from the bowl and shape it into a flat round on an oiled baking sheet. Press or roll the dough out to a circle about 10 inches in diameter. Press down on the center of the dough slightly, and make a 9-inch central portion indented just a bit to receive the topping.

Mix the egg and oregano into the cooked vegetables. Spread the mixture over the indented portion of the bread, arranging the pepper artistically in the process. Sprinkle with salt and grind on a bit of pepper. Let the bread rise for 30 minutes. Preheat the oven to 350°F.

Bake for 45 to 50 minutes, or until the bread sounds hollow when tapped on the bottom.

Boxty Bread

Makes 1 loaf

1 pound (3 medium large) all-purpose potatoes, peeled	⅛ teaspoon freshly ground pepper
1 package yeast	2 cups cooked mashed potatoes
4 tablespoons melted butter	About 7 cups unbleached flour
2 teaspoons salt	

Grate the potatoes, preferably with a hand grater. Place a sieve over a bowl and, taking up handfuls of the potatoes, squeeze them over the sieve to expel excess liquid. Measure the liquid and add water, if necessary, to make ¼ cup. Dissolve the yeast in it.

In a large bowl, mix the yeast, butter, salt, pepper, mashed potatoes, and grated potatoes. Work in a goodly amount of flour, enough so that you can turn the bread out from its bowl and onto a floured counter. Knead well and heartily for 10 minutes, adding flour as necessary, until a firm dough forms. This dough tends to be sticky, so continue kneading in flour until the dough no longer sticks to hands or board. Put the dough in an oiled bowl and let rise in a warm place for 1½ hours. (The dough will seem sluggish.)

Scatter a thick covering of flour on a work surface, remove the dough from the bowl, and rub one surface of the dough in the flour

The traditional recipe for Irish Boxty Bread calls for no yeast and results in a deliciously flavored but impossibly heavy loaf. This yeasted version is still a good sturdy bread, and it has all the fresh potato taste of the original. The crust is particularly crisp and delectable. This is wonderful dipped in garlic butter, but then, so is almost anything.

until it is heavily coated. Round the dough and place it, floured side up, on an oiled baking sheet. With kitchen shears, snip 4 dividing lines across the surface so that the bread divides evenly into 8 wedge-shaped sections or, as the Irish say, "farls."

Bake the bread for 1 hour, or until it makes a clean hollow sound when you knock the bottom of the loaf with your fist. Serve slightly warm, with plenty of unsalted butter.

Forest Mushroom Bread with Mushroom Butter

Makes 1 large loaf or 2 small loaves
(Color plate 19)

Buckwheat, molasses, Cognac, dried mushrooms—all the musty, fungal flavors I could think of—combine to make this a particularly interesting essence bread. Dried mushroom powder is available in most specialty food stores in the pasta section, next to pasta flour. All the powdered vegetables (carrot, spinach, mushroom, and tomato) that are used to flavor homemade pastas are also amusing to experiment with in breads.

1½ ounces dried mushrooms (Shiitaki or European mushrooms)
1 pound fresh mushrooms, cleaned, trimmed, and finely chopped
4 tablespoons unsalted butter
1 package yeast
2 tablespoons finely grated onion
1 tablespoon molasses
2 tablespoons buckwheat flour
1 tablespoon dried mushroom powder (optional)
1 tablespoon Cognac
2 teaspoons salt
Several grinds of fresh pepper
About 3⅓ cups unbleached flour

Bring 1½ cups water and the dried mushrooms to a boil. Remove from heat, cover the pot, and let the mushrooms sit for 20 minutes to soften.

Place a sieve over a bowl. Squeeze the fresh chopped mushrooms over the sieve and reserve the mushroom liquid. Melt the butter in a frying pan and sauté the chopped mushrooms over high heat until they are cooked and dry in the pan. Reserve 2 tablespoons mushrooms for the Mushroom Butter.

Drain the dried mushrooms, reserving the water, and squeeze them to remove all the water. Combine the dried mushroom water and fresh mushroom water in a measuring cup. Add enough water to bring the total amount to 1¼ cups. Finely chop the dried mushrooms and add them to the sautéed fresh mushrooms. (If you are using Shiitaki mushrooms, discard the tough stems.)

Put the mushroom water in a large bowl; add the yeast and stir until dissolved. Add the onion, molasses, buckwheat flour, mushroom powder, Cognac, salt, pepper, and mushrooms, and stir. Stir in 3 cups flour to form a dough that can be turned out onto a floured kneading surface. Continue to knead for 10 minutes, adding more flour as necessary, until a smooth, unsticky dough forms. Put the dough in an oiled bowl, cover, and let rise in a warm place for 1 hour, or until doubled in bulk.

Preheat the oven to 350°F. Form the dough into 1 large round or 2 small rounds (Mushroom Bread works well as a basket bread; see page 13), or form in 2 large loaf pans. Let rise for about 45 minutes, or until nearly doubled. If you wish to experiment with mushroom shapes, try baking breads in soufflé molds or small dariole molds for individual mushroom-shaped breads. Bake for 1 hour for large breads, about 45 minutes for small breads.

Mushroom Butter

8 tablespoons (1 stick) unsalted butter, softened
2 tablespoons sautéed mushrooms
½ teaspoon dried mushroom powder (optional)
Drop or 2 of lemon juice

Salt to taste
Freshly ground pepper
A knife tip of mashed garlic
Pinch confectioners' sugar, if necessary
1 large sautéed fluted mushroom (optional) for garnish

Combine all ingredients except the sugar and cream to a smooth blend. Taste and add more salt, pepper, and lemon juice if needed. If the butter seems bitter, add the merest pinches of sugar until it is pleasingly balanced. Heap the butter into a serving dish and top, if you wish, with a handsome fluted mushroom.

Swirled Parmesan Bread

Makes 1 large wheel or 2 small wheels

2 packages yeast
1⅓ cups warm water
4 tablespoons melted unsalted butter
1 teaspoon sugar
1½ teaspoons salt
4 cups all-purpose flour

For the cheese topping

3 eggs
2 tablespoons melted unsalted butter
1 teaspoon paprika
2 large garlic cloves, pressed
Freshly ground pepper
1¼ cups grated Parmesan cheese

A *pretty, sunny-looking bread with a crisp Parmesan crust. This is excellent served with red wine.*

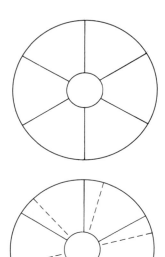

Dissolve the yeast in warm water. Add the melted butter, sugar, and salt, then add around 3½ cups of the flour. Knead briefly, then turn out onto a floured work surface. Continue kneading for 8 minutes, adding the remaining flour, until a firm dough results. Put the dough in an oiled bowl, cover with a towel, and let rise in a warm place for 1 hour.

To make the topping, beat the eggs in a bowl until well blended. Add melted butter, paprika, garlic, and several grinds of pepper and mix well. Stir in the grated cheese.

Roll the dough out to a circle a generous 1 inch thick for a large bread, ¾ inch thick for small breads. Transfer to an oiled baking pan. Leaving 2 inches uncut at the center, cut lines through the dough from center to edge. Give each cut portion a half twist and overlap the slices slightly. Let rise for 15 minutes, then thickly spread the cheese mixture on the interior of each "petal," leaving some of the bread along the rim of each section white in contrast. Let rise for another 30 minutes.

Preheat the oven to 350°F. Bake for 45 to 50 minutes for a large loaf, 30 minutes for the small loaves. The topping should be deep golden and crusty; the bread should sound hollow when tapped on the bottom. Serve warm.

Mustard Bread

Makes 1 loaf

I adore this unusual bread. It is a gorgeous pale mustard color, it stays moist and succulent, and it is absolutely perfect when spread with a mayonnaise-mustard mix and topped with ham. This is also delicious simply topped with one of the fine, exotic mustard butters or honey mustards available in gourmet shops.

1 medium onion, chopped
2 tablespoons butter
1 package yeast
1 tablespoon sugar
½ cup warm water
½ cup milk, warm
1 teaspoon salt
¼ teaspoon turmeric
3 tablespoons Dijon-style mustard

2 tablespoons coarse-grained mustard
Freshly ground pepper
1 egg (reserve half the yolk)
About 4⅓ cups unbleached flour

For the glaze
Reserved egg yolk
2 teaspoons coarse-grained mustard

In a covered frying pan, cook the onion in butter over low heat until it is very soft. Purée in a blender or food processor.

In a large bowl, dissolve the yeast and sugar in warm water. Add onion, milk, salt, turmeric, both mustards, the several grinds of fresh pepper, and the egg (reserving half of the yolk). Mix well. Add flour until a cohesive dough forms that can be turned out of the bowl. Knead for 10 minutes, adding flour as necessary, until a medium-firm dough develops. Put the dough in an oiled bowl, cover with a towel, and leave to rise in a warm place for 1 hour. (The dough may seem a bit sluggish.)

Remove dough from the bowl and place in a buttered 9 x 5 x 3-inch loaf pan. Let the dough rise again in a warm place for about 40 minutes, until it gently mounds over the top of the pan.

Preheat the oven to 350°F.

Mix the reserved half egg yolk, mustard, and a few drops of water. Brush glaze over the bread. Bake the bread for about 50 minutes. Unmold the bread and let it cool on a rack.

Baked Potato Breads with Sour Cream and Chives

Makes 2 large loaves or 8 individual rolls
(Color plate 15)

1½ packages yeast
¼ cup warm water
½ cup sour cream
2 tablespoons buttermilk
2 tablespoons melted unsalted
   butter
1 tablespoon sugar
2 teaspoons salt
1 egg, lightly beaten
1 ounce (⅔ cup) dried mashed
   potato flakes

½ cup mixed finely chopped
   chives or white and tender
   green portion of green onions
1 teaspoon baking powder
About 5½ cups all-purpose flour

For the glaze
1 tablespoon rice flour or
   cornstarch
1 tablespoon flour
¼ teaspoon salt

In a large bowl, dissolve the yeast in warm water. Stir in the sour cream, buttermilk, melted butter, sugar, salt, egg, and mashed potato flakes and mix well. Stir in chives. Sprinkle on the baking powder and stir in enough flour to make a dough firm enough to turn out onto a floured kneading surface. Knead a good 10 or 12 minutes, adding flour until the bread no longer feels sticky (though the dough will be rather soft). Put the dough in a greased bowl and turn the dough so the top will be oiled also. Cover and let rise in a warm spot for about 1½ hours, until doubled in bulk.

Gently remove the dough from the bowl and divide it into two portions, for large bread, or 8 portions, for individual rolls. Gently elongate the dough and shape each portion roughly into a long, 10-

This most amusing recipe will delight guests. Imagine two huge potatoes brought to the table, stuffed with slabs of butter and dollops of sour cream, that turn out to be tasty potato bread. Serve these with a serrated knife alongside, and let guests cut their own portions and dip into the creamy goodness of melting cream and butter. This recipe can also be turned into individual potato rolls, to serve with a luncheon salad and a round of Brie.

inch potato shape (or a 4- to 5-inch-long "potato" for rolls). Put the breads on an oiled baking sheet, cover, and let rise for 15 minutes.

Mix the rice flour (or cornstarch) and flour in a frying pan. Put over medium heat and stir continuously until the flour is toasted a medium brown. Do not burn. Put the flour in a cup. Stir in the salt and a generous 2 tablespoons water until a thin paste results. Brush the paste over the breads. Using scissors, cut a 5-inch slit to the depth of 1 inch down the middle of each bread and gently push the dough open (this will be the white "potato meal" portion showing through the "skin"). Cut a small strip of aluminum foil and lay it over each white portion. Let bread rise for another 15 minutes. Preheat the oven to 350°F.

Bake the breads for 45 to 50 minutes. They should sound hollow when tapped on the bottom. Remove from the oven. Let cool briefly, then place each bread on a sheet of aluminum foil and bunch the foil around the bread for decorative effect. Cut the center of each "potato" and insert two or three large slabs of butter. Spoon on some extra sour cream, sprinkle with additional chives if you wish, and serve warm. (This bread can be made ahead and reheated in foil if you desire.)

Savory Walnut Bread with Goat Cheese Butter

Makes 1 loaf

This is an unsweet nut bread meant to accompany salads and cheeses. It is particularly delicious with goat cheese and delicate salads of the nouvelle *persuasion that contain rustic greens like radicchio and arugula. The walnut exterior is a nice touch, as it bakes into a crisp enrobing crust.*

1 package yeast
2 teaspoons sugar
1½ cups warm water
2 tablespoons walnut oil
2 teaspoons salt
2 tablespoons finely grated onion
1 cup pulverized English
   (California) walnuts
Generous 3½ cups unbleached
   flour

For the nut crust

1 egg
⅔ cup pulverized walnuts
¼ teaspoon salt
2 tablespoons unbleached flour
Walnut oil
7 whole walnut halves

Dissolve the yeast and sugar in warm water. Stir in the walnut oil, salt, onion, and walnuts. Begin adding flour, a cup at a time. Mix well until the dough can be turned out onto a floured surface. Knead for 10 minutes, adding flour as necessary, until the dough is no longer sticky. Oil a bowl (preferably with walnut oil), put dough in the bowl, turning it to oil its entire surface, then cover with a towel and set in a warm place to rise for 1 hour.

Oil a baking sheet. Take the dough from the bowl and put it on the sheet. Press the dough and stretch it with your hands into a rough round shape 1½ inches thick. Cover and let rise for 30 minutes in a warm spot.

To prepare topping, in a small bowl mix together the egg, walnuts, salt, flour, and 1 tablespoon water. Spread the mixture over the bread with a knife or spatula. Smooth the mixture over the sides of the bread right down to the baking sheet. Gently press 8 indentations into the bread with a finger. Fill the indentations with walnut oil. Arrange walnut halves on top of the bread, one in the center, six others around it. Let the bread rise 30 to 40 minutes before baking.

Bake the bread in a 350° oven for 45 to 50 minutes. The bottom of the loaf should sound hollow when knocked with a fist.

Let the bread cool and serve with Goat Cheese Butter.

Goat Cheese Butter

3 ounces unsalted butter, softened
2 ounces cream cheese
2 ounces mild soft goat cheese, such as Boucheron

1 tablespoon coarsely chopped walnuts
Freshly ground pepper
Salt to taste
1 large walnut half

Cream together the butter, cream cheese, and goat cheese. Stir in the walnuts and a few grinds of fresh pepper and taste to see if extra salt is needed. Mound onto a serving dish and garnish with the walnut half.

Fresh Apple Bread with Apple Butter

Makes 1 loaf

3 medium-large apples
2 tablespoons lemon juice
1 cup sugar
1 stick unsalted butter, softened
2 eggs
1½ tablespoons buttermilk
1 teaspoon vanilla extract
½ teaspoon salt
¼ teaspoon ginger

1 teaspoon cinnamon
¾ cup finely chopped dried apples
1 teaspoon baking powder
2 cups all-purpose flour

For the syrup
⅓ cup apple juice or cider
1 cup light brown sugar, packed

This is a fragrant, full-of-fresh-fruit-tasting bread that is as close to apple essence as is possible to make. Serve the bread with commercial apple butter.

Peel and core the apples. Put them and the lemon juice in a blender or food processor and process to a purée. Set aside.

Preheat the oven to 325°F. Butter a 9 x 5 x 3-inch loaf pan.

Using a mixer, cream together the sugar and butter. Add the eggs and beat until well blended. Stir in the apples, buttermilk, vanilla, salt, ginger, cinnamon, and dried apples. Sprinkle the baking powder over the batter, then add flour and stir until perfectly mixed. Spoon batter into the loaf pan. Bake for 1 hour, then check the bread for doneness by inserting a wooden skewer at its center. If it seems at all wet, bake the bread for another 5 to 10 minutes.

About 15 minutes before the bread is to come out of the oven, put the apple juice and ½ cup brown sugar in a pan and bring to a simmer. Simmer for 5 minutes.

Take the bread from the oven and immediately sprinkle it with 3 tablespoons brown sugar. Drizzle apple syrup on the top and sides. Alternate sprinkling sugar and drizzling syrup twice more, to form a chewy, sugary crust. Let the bread cool for 10 minutes, then gently turn it out of the pan. Let it sit for at least 2 hours before cutting.

Serve with apple butter.

Gingered Banana Bread with Rum Butter

A banana bread with a difference! Ginger, toasted coconut, and banana chips combine to make this a most sophisticated version of an old favorite.

Makes 1 large loaf

1 cup sugar
8 tablespoons (1 stick) butter, softened
2 eggs
1 cup puréed bananas (around 3 to 3½ medium bananas)
1½ tablespoons buttermilk
2 tablespoons lemon juice
½ teaspoon salt
¼ teaspoon ground ginger
½ cup toasted flaked coconut
⅓ cup crumbled dried banana chips

2 tablespoons finely chopped crystallized ginger (optional)
1 teaspoon baking powder
2 cups all-purpose flour

For the syrup
¼ cup dark or light brown sugar
1 tablespoon butter
1 tablespoon rum, preferably dark

Butter a 9 x 5 x 3-inch loaf pan. Preheat the oven to 325°F.

Cream together the sugar and butter. Stir in the eggs, then add banana purée, buttermilk, and lemon juice, and mix well. Add salt, ground ginger, coconut, banana chips, and crystallized ginger. Sprinkle the baking powder over the surface, then rapidly stir in the flour and mix everything until perfectly blended. Spoon into buttered loaf pan and put in the oven to bake for 1 hour. Test the center of the bread with a wooden skewer to see if it is done. If it comes out damp, the bread may need an additional 5 to 10 minutes of baking. Remove from the oven and let bread cool in the pan while you prepare syrup.

Combine brown sugar and ¼ cup water in a pan and simmer for 5 minutes. Turn off the heat and stir in the butter, then rum. With a skewer, poke holes all over the surface of the bread and particularly close to the edges. Spoon syrup over the bread and down the sides in several batches. Don't just douse the center; pay particular attention to the edges. Let the bread absorb the syrup for 10 minutes, then gently unmold the bread. Let cool before cutting. Serve with Rum Butter.

Rum Butter

8 tablespoons (1 stick) unsalted
  butter, softened
1 tablespoon confectioners' sugar
1 tablespoon brown sugar, lump-
  free

Pinch ginger
1 tablespoon rum, or to taste

Cream all the ingredients together until a smooth butter results. Mound into a butter dish and serve at spreading consistency.

Pistachio Lemon Bread
with Lemon Butter

Makes 1 loaf
(Color plate 20)

2 lemons
1½ cups sugar
¾ cup pistachios, shelled
¾ cup (1½ sticks) unsalted
  butter, softened
3 eggs
2¼ cups all-purpose flour
½ teaspoon salt

¼ teaspoon baking soda
½ cup buttermilk
¼ cup lemon juice

For the glaze
⅓ cup sugar
Juice of 1 lemon

A lovely pale yellow bread studded with green pistachios and briskly, abundantly flavored with lemon. Serve with teas or with a fruit salad lunch.

Cut large thick strips of zest from one of the lemons. Put the sugar in a bowl and add the zest. Work the sugar and zest together with your fingers to impregnate the sugar with lemon flavor. Set aside. Finely grate the zest from the other lemon and reserve.

Bring a small pan of water to a boil. Add the pistachios. Boil for 1 minute, then remove from the heat and let sit for 5 minutes. Drain the nuts. Put them in a clean but not valuable dish towel and rub them firmly to loosen their skins. Remove skins, then coarsely break up the nuts.

Preheat the oven to 350°F. Butter and flour a 9 x 5 x 3-inch loaf pan. Remove the zest from the sugar, scrape off any sugar that adheres to it, and reserve zest for the Lemon Butter. Cream the flavored sugar and butter together until light and fluffy. Add the eggs, one at a time, and beat until light.

In a large bowl, combine the pistachio nuts, flour, salt, and grated zest.

In another bowl, stir together the baking soda and buttermilk and stir into the creamed butter, along with the lemon juice. Add the flour mixture and stir gently just until the ingredients are perfectly blended. Spoon into the prepared pan. Bake for about 1 hour and 10 minutes. Cover the bread with foil during the baking if it threatens to overbrown. The bread is done when a wooden skewer stuck in the center comes out clean.

Shortly before the bread is to come from the oven, make the glaze. Combine the sugar, lemon juice, and ⅓ cup water in a pan. Bring to a simmer and cook for 4 minutes.

When the bread comes from the oven, immediately poke holes all over the top with a wooden skewer. Spoon the glaze over the bread and down the sides. Let the bread remain in the pan for 10 minutes, then carefully turn it out onto a cooling rack. Let it cool to room temperature before cutting. Serve with Lemon Butter.

Lemon Butter

8 tablespoons (1 stick) butter, softened

2 tablespoons confectioners' sugar
1 teaspoon reserved lemon zest, minced

Cream together the butter, confectioners' sugar, and zest. Mound into a serving bowl.

Pear Loaf with Macadamia Nuts

Makes 1 loaf

2 large ripe pears, peeled
1 tablespoon lemon juice
8 tablespoons (1 stick) unsalted
    butter, softened
1 cup sugar
2 eggs
2 tablespoons buttermilk
1 teaspoon vanilla extract
½ teaspoon salt
1 teaspoon ginger
1 tablespoon Poire (pear liqueur)
    or light rum
¼ cup pear jam
1 cup dried pears, cut into
    ¼-inch dice

½ cup quartered macadamia
    nuts
1½ teaspoons baking powder
2 cups all-purpose flour

For the topping

1 glacéed pear half, diced
    (optional)

For the glaze

¼ cup sugar
1 tablespoon pear jam
1 tablespoon Poire or light rum

This fruit-filled loaf has a complex and interesting texture. The dried pears add almost a crisp fresh-fruit consistency, and the macadamias provide a soft nutty counterpoint. Serve with a good pear jam or butter.

Preheat the oven to 350°F. Butter a 9 x 5 x 3-inch loaf pan.

Purée the pears and lemon juice and set aside. Cream the butter and sugar, then stir in the eggs, buttermilk, vanilla, salt, ginger, Poire, jam, and puréed pears. Mix well. Add the dried pears and nuts, and when well blended, sprinkle baking powder over the top. Stir in the flour. Mix until just blended, then spoon into the loaf pan. Sprinkle the top with diced glacéed pear, if desired.

Bake for 1¼ hours. Test with a wooden skewer toward the end of baking time and make sure the center of the loaf is not wet. Cover with aluminum foil if the top threatens to overbrown.

Just before the bread is done, prepare the glaze. Bring sugar, jam, and ¼ cup water to a boil, then simmer for 5 minutes. Off the heat, stir in the Poire.

Take bread from the oven, poke a few 1-inch-deep holes with a skewer, spoon half the glaze over the bread, and let the other half drip down the sides.

Let cool before turning out of the pan.

Orange Marmalade Bread
with Orange Butter

Makes 1 loaf

I tested several orange breads before hitting upon one that seemed to me sufficiently "orangey." The trick is to use orange marmalade as a flavoring. Choose the jar that seems to have the most peel floating in it.

2 large oranges
1 cup sugar
¾ cup (1½ sticks) unsalted butter, at room temperature
3 eggs
¼ cup freshly squeezed orange juice
½ cup orange marmalade
1 teaspoon vanilla extract
2 tablespoons Grand Marnier, or other orange liqueur

½ teaspoon salt
½ cup slivered blanched almonds
⅓ cup buttermilk
¼ teaspoon baking soda
2¼ cups all-purpose flour

For the glaze

¼ cup sugar
2 tablespoons orange marmalade
1 tablespoon Grand Marnier

Cut 3 long wide strips of zest from one of the oranges and reserve. Finely grate the remaining zest from this orange and from the second orange. Reserve ½ teaspoon finely grated zest for the Orange Butter.

Butter and flour a 9 x 5 x 3-inch loaf pan. Preheat the oven to 350°F.

Put the grated zest (except for the reserved ½ teaspoon) in a bowl and add the sugar. Rub them together for 2 or 3 minutes to impart orange flavor to the sugar. Add the softened butter, and cream together until light and fluffy.

Stir in the eggs, one at a time, then add the orange juice, marmalade, vanilla, Grand Marnier, salt, and almonds and mix well.

Stir the buttermilk and soda together, then add to the batter. Stir in the flour gently, and when everything is thoroughly blended (do not overbeat), pour batter into the prepared pan.

Bake at 350°F for approximately 45 minutes. Reduce the heat to 325°F and bake for another 30 minutes. (Test for doneness with a wooden skewer.) During the last 30 or so minutes of baking, cover the top of the loaf with aluminum foil to prevent it from overbrowning.

Five minutes before the bread is to come from the oven, prepare the glaze. Combine the reserved strips of zest, sugar, marmalade, and ¼ cup water in a saucepan. Simmer for 5 minutes; tamp down frequently on the zest to release its flavor. Turn off the heat, discard the zest, and add the Grand Marnier.

Take the bread from the oven; with a skewer dot the top with a series of small holes, and spoon the glaze over the top. Let the bread cool before turning it out from the pan. Serve with Orange Butter.

Orange Butter

8 tablespoons (1 stick) unsalted
   butter, softened
1 tablespoon orange marmalade

1 tablespoon confectioners' sugar
½ teaspoon reserved grated zest
1 tablespoon Grand Marnier

Cream together all ingredients and mound in a serving dish.

Pumpkin Pie Loaves
with Cinnamon Butter

Makes 1 large or 2 small loaves

These festive, beautifully colored loaves are evocative reminders of Thanksgiving at any time of year.

1½ packages yeast
¼ cup warm water
½ cup milk
¾ cup dark brown sugar
2 tablespoons butter
1½ teaspoons salt
1 egg, lightly beaten
1 pound canned pumpkin purée,
   or 2 cups freshly made purée
Scant ¼ teaspoon nutmeg
½ teaspoon ground ginger
¼ teaspoon cinnamon
Large pinch ground cloves

Large pinch mace
2 tablespoons crystallized ginger,
   minced (optional)
4¼ to 4½ cups all-purpose flour

For the topping

⅔ cup brown sugar
½ teaspoon cinnamon
Pinch salt
6 tablespoons unsalted butter,
   softened
⅓ cup plus 2 tablespoons flour

Dissolve the yeast in warm water. Put the milk, brown sugar, butter, and salt in a saucepan and heat until the butter and sugar have melted. Remove from the heat and let cool. Mix with the yeast, egg, and pumpkin purée.

Measure the spices and crystallized ginger into a large bowl. Add 3 cups flour and stir until well blended. Make a well in the center and add the liquid ingredients. Mix, and sprinkle in more flour until you are able to turn the dough from the bowl. Knead for 10 minutes, adding flour as necessary, until the dough is soft but not sticky. Put in an oiled bowl, cover with a towel, and let rise in a warm place for about 1 hour, or until doubled in bulk. Form into 1 large loaf or 2 small loaves and put in a buttered loaf pan. Let rise again for 30 minutes.

Preheat the oven to 350°F.

To make the topping, mix together the brown sugar, cinnamon, salt, butter, and flour. With your fingers or a fork, mix until crumbly and well blended. Scatter the topping over the bread.

Bake for 50 minutes for a large loaf, 35 to 40 minutes for small loaves. Serve with Cinnamon Butter.

Cinnamon Butter

8 tablespoons (1 stick) unsalted butter, softened
2 tablespoons sifted confectioners' sugar

¼ teaspoon cinnamon, or to taste

Cream together the butter, confectioners' sugar, and cinnamon. Taste and add more sugar or cinnamon if you desire. Mound the butter on a serving dish.

Chocolate Chip Bread with Chocolate Nut Butter

Makes 1 loaf

This bread is slow to rise but quick to be devoured. Slather on Chocolate Butter and you will have a true treat for chocolate lovers.

1 package yeast
½ cup warm water
½ cup sugar
3 ounces white chocolate
½ cup warm milk
1 tablespoon plus 1 teaspoon cocoa

½ teaspoon salt
About 3⅓ cups all-purpose flour
¾ cup semisweet chocolate mini-morsels
⅓ cup chopped pecans

Dissolve the yeast in warm water in a medium-sized bowl. Add the sugar.

Melt white chocolate in a double boiler over hot water. Add the warm milk, let cool briefly, then add to the yeast. Stir well.

Sift together the cocoa, salt, and 3 cups flour together in a large bowl. Make a well in the center, then add the liquid, stirring continuously. Add the chocolate morsels and nuts and knead until the dough can be turned out onto a floured work surface. Knead for about 10 minutes, adding the remaining ⅓ cup or so flour as necessary. Knead until the dough is smooth and elastic. Put in a greased bowl, cover with a towel, and put in a warm area to rise for 1½ hours. (Do not expect great dough volume.)

Punch down and put in a buttered 9 x 5 x 3-inch loaf pan. Let the dough rise again for about 1 hour, or until it reaches over the top of the pan. If the dough is terribly sluggish, place it briefly on a warm surface, such as a casserole inverted over a warm stove burner.

Preheat the oven to 350°F. Bake the bread for 50 minutes. Turn out and let cool completely before spreading with Chocolate Butter.

Chocolate Butter

8 tablespoons (1 stick) unsalted butter, softened
2 ounces semisweet chocolate, melted and cooled

½ cup finely chopped toasted pecans

Stir together the butter, chocolate, and pecans. Scoop into a serving dish, and serve at room temperature so butter does not harden.

Toasted Almond Bread with Amaretto Butter

Makes 1 large loaf

1½ sticks unsalted butter, softened
2 large eggs
7 ounces almond paste, cut into pieces
1 teaspoon almond extract
⅓ cup warm water
½ teaspoon salt

½ teaspoon baking soda
½ cup buttermilk
1 cup coarsely chopped toasted almonds
2 cups unbleached flour
Amaretto liqueur
Confectioners' sugar

This is a bread thoroughly almond in flavor, and excellent for either tea or toasting. It also makes a good holiday bread even though it looks humble in appearance.

Butter and flour a 9 x 5 x 3-inch loaf pan. Preheat the oven to 325°F.

Cream together the butter, eggs, and almond paste. When well blended, add the almond extract, warm water, and salt, and continue to mix until smooth. Dissolve the baking soda in the buttermilk, then add to the butter mixture. Stir in the almonds and finally the flour. Scrape the batter into the prepared pan and lightly smooth it even.

Bake for 1 hour. Test with a wooden skewer; if it comes out wet, bake for an additional 5 to 10 minutes. As the bread comes from the oven, sprinkle the top generously with Amaretto, then powder the top heavily with confectioners' sugar shaken from a sifter.

Let the bread cool for 10 minutes, then turn the loaf out carefully, and continue shaking on confectioners' sugar until the top is white and thickly coated. Let cool completely before slicing. Serve with Amaretto Butter.

Amaretto Butter

8 tablespoons (1 stick) unsalted butter, softened
2 tablespoons confectioners' sugar
1½ tablespoons Amaretto, or to taste

3 tablespoons finely chopped toasted almonds

Cream together the butter, confectioners' sugar, Amaretto, and almonds. Mound in a serving dish.

SWEET AND FESTIVE BREADS

*At length I recollected the thoughtless
saying of a great princess, who, on being
informed that the country people had no
bread, replied, "Let them eat cake."*
Jean Jacques Rousseau

Nothing is more delicious than warm rolls encrusted with cinnamon and sugar and buns sticky with caramel. Here are a variety of sweet breads—long twists as professional-looking as any commercial baker's; a huge cinnamon sticky bun drizzled with sugar glaze; Moravian Sugar Bread with pockets of crisp buttery sweetness. A most unusual festive bread from Italy twists itself into a benign "serpent" with a raisin smile and a coat of brightly colored sprinkles. I think for all out glamour, nothing can top the intricately patterned Della Robbia Wreath as a holiday attraction.

For the "Let them eat cake" fanciers, I've added the fastest recipe for brioche I have ever made. (Marie Antoinette *did* mean brioche when she said cake—not such a bad fate after all if the brioche is sweet and feather-light.)

Challah

Makes 2 loaves

The beautiful braided Jewish egg bread, challah, possesses an elegantly rich exterior and a golden, slightly chewy interior. It never fails to delight guests, and it makes a much appreciated holiday gift.

1 package yeast
2 tablespoons sugar
1⅓ cups warm water
Around 5 cups unbleached flour
2 teaspoons salt
2 tablespoons vegetable oil
2 eggs, lightly beaten

For the glaze
1 egg yolk beaten with 2
  teaspoons water

For the topping
1 tablespoon poppy seeds

Dissolve the yeast and sugar in ⅓ cup of the warm water.

Mix 4 cups flour and the salt in a large mixing bowl. Make a well in the center. Add yeast, the remaining 1 cup warm water, the vegetable oil, and the eggs. Stir and combine the dough until it is firm enough to be turned out onto a floured work surface. Knead, adding the rest of the flour as necessary, until the dough is no longer sticky. Continue to knead for about 8 minutes until the dough is medium-firm and elastic. Put the dough in a clean, lightly oiled bowl, cover with a towel, and leave to rise in a warm spot for 1 hour.

Punch the dough down well to remove all air bubbles. Form the dough into a ball, cover, and let rise again for about 45 minutes, or until doubled in bulk. This second rising is what gives the bread its finely grained, springy texture.

When the dough has risen again to double its bulk, turn it out onto a board and divide it in half. Cover one half with plastic wrap and set aside.

Divide the remaining half into 3 portions for a 3-strand braid, or 4 portions for a 4-strand braid (see following instructions). Squeeze (rather than stretch) and roll the portions into long ropes. (For a 3-strand braid, the ropes will be 20 inches long.) Break any large air bubbles. When the ropes are smooth and of sufficient length, braid the bread. Place the finished braid on one side of an oiled baking sheet and cover lightly with a towel. Braid the remaining portion of dough and set it on the baking sheet.

Let the braided breads rise for approximately 1 hour, or until doubled in bulk. Brush the loaves with egg yolk glaze and sprinkle with poppy seeds.

Bake in a preheated 350°F oven for 35 to 40 minutes, or until the loaves sound hollow when rapped on the bottom with a fist.

To Make a 4-Strand Braid

Divide the dough into 4 portions and roll and squeeze each until it forms a smooth 10-inch-long rope, then elongate each rope by rolling it back and forth under your palms until it is 20 inches long.

Step 1: Lay the strands out in the shape of a large **X**, with each strand radiating out from the center. Gently pinch the ends together at the center to form a temporary attachment.

Step 2: With your right hand holding A and left hand holding B, cross the right arm over the left so that A crosses over B, and at the same time, both cross over C.

Step 3: Now reverse the procedure. Hold C in your right hand and D in your left hand. Cross your left hand over your right, so that D crosses over C and both cross over A.

Step 4: Hold B in your right hand and A in your left hand. Cross your right hand over the left, and at the same time, cross both strands over D.

Step 5: With D in your right hand and C in your left, cross your left hand over the right and both strands over B.

Repeat these steps until the braid is complete. Pinch the ends together and tuck them under the braid.

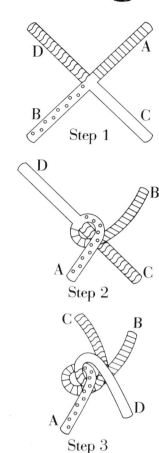

Christmas Cider Nut Bread

Makes 1 loaf

8 tablespoons (1 stick) unsalted butter, softened

¾ cup sugar

3 eggs, separated

½ cup plus 1 tablespoon apple cider

2½ cups all-purpose flour

⅔ cup mixed candied cherries and pineapple

¼ teaspoon grated lemon zest

⅔ cup pecans

½ cup raisins

1 teaspoon salt

1 tablespoon baking powder

This delicious and relatively quick holiday fruit bread is somewhat unusual in its composition.

Butter a 9 x 5 x 3-inch bread pan.

In a bowl, cream together the butter and ½ cup sugar. Stir in the egg yolks and apple cider. Set aside.

Place ½ cup flour in a bowl. Add candied fruit, lemon zest, pecans, and raisins and mix well.

Sift the remaining 2 cups flour together with the salt and baking powder.

Beat the egg whites until they start to stiffen, then gradually beat in the remaining ¼ cup sugar. Continue beating until very stiff.

To assemble the bread, stir the fruit and nut mixture into the creamed butter. Stir in the sifted flour. Thoroughly mix in half the egg whites, then fold in the remaining whites. Pour the batter into the prepared pan. Let stand for 20 minutes.

Preheat the oven to 350°F. Bake the bread for 60 minutes, or until a toothpick inserted into the center of the bread comes out completely dry. Let the bread cool for 10 minutes before turning it out of the pan. This may be served plain or frosted with a simple confectioners' icing (see page 108), if desired.

Brioche

Makes 1 large brioche or 2 small brioches

2 tablespoons sugar
6 eggs
2 tablespoons milk
¾ teaspoon vanilla extract
1 package yeast
1 teaspoon salt
3 cups bread flour

8 tablespoons (1 stick) butter, well softened

For the glaze
1 egg yolk beaten with 2 teaspoons water

Here is a recipe for the fastest brioche you will probably ever find. It utilizes, surprisingly, bromated bread flour and a long machine kneading. The result is a gossamer-light, uniformly crumbed, impeccable brioche.

Combine the sugar, eggs, milk, and vanilla in a heatproof metal mixing bowl, or saucepan. Place the bowl or pan over low heat and warm the ingredients, stirring them constantly with your hand so that you can feel when the eggs turn pleasantly warm, but do not heat to the point where they are in danger of scrambling. Remove the egg mixture from heat and transfer to an electric mixer.

Stir the yeast into the egg mixture. Let sit for 2 minutes. Add salt and flour then beat for 10 minutes with a dough hook or kneading blade. Stop the machine every 2 minutes and scrape down the bowl.

While the machine continues to beat, add in the butter, a tablespoon at a time. Beat for another 4 minutes, until the dough is very smooth and elastic.

Put the dough in a clean, buttered bowl. Cover with a towel and let rise in a warm place for 1 hour.

Generously butter a brioche mold. To make a classic *brioche à tête,* lightly flour your hands, remove the damp dough from its rising bowl, pinch off a generous quarter of the dough and set aside.

Place the large dough portion in the buttered brioche mold. Insert 2 fingers in the dough, slightly off center, to make a deep indentation. Reflour your hands and form the small portion of dough into a round with one pointed end. Set the point down into the indentation you have made.

Brush the bread with the egg yolk glaze, cover, and set in a warm place to rise for about 45 minutes, or until the dough comes within ½ inch of the top of the mold.

Bake in a preheated 350°F oven for about 50 minutes. The bread will rise 3 to 4 inches during baking, so be sure to bake on a low enough rack to allow for this expansion.

Umbrian "Serpent" Bread

Makes 1 large serpent bread

5 cups all-purpose flour
2 envelopes yeast
¼ cup warm water
⅓ cup warm milk
2 tablespoons melted butter
2 teaspoons orange-flower water
1½ teaspoons salt
¼ cup sugar
½ teaspoon ginger
¼ teaspoon cinnamon
4 eggs
1 medium apple, peeled, cored, grated, and squeezed to remove excess juice
Zest of 1 lemon, grated

Zest of 1 large orange, grated
¼ cup golden raisins
¼ cup dark raisins
½ cup pine nuts, coarsely chopped

For the glaze
1 egg yolk beaten with 2 teaspoons water and ¼ teaspoon sugar

For the trim
Dark raisins
Colored sugar
Candy confetti

This funny festive bread, with its pine nuts, raisins, and faint orange-flower water aroma, is a most typical Italian sweet loaf. Its twining serpent shape is traditional in the region of Umbria. Sprinkle the creature liberally with colored sugar crystals and candy confetti, and grace him with a benign raisin smile.

Put 1½ cups flour in the mixing bowl of an electric mixer, sprinkle with yeast, and stir well. Add warm water and milk, melted butter, orange-flower water, salt, sugar, and spices and begin to mix. Break in the eggs, one at a time, and blend each one in at low speed, beating until the dough is smooth after each addition. Mix in the apple and orange and lemon zest. Add 2 cups flour. Beat for 3 minutes on medium-high speed.

Sprinkle the remaining flour over the dough, then turn the dough out and continue kneading in the flour by hand. Knead for about 5 minutes, or until the dough is smooth and elastic. Put in an oiled bowl, cover, and let rise in a warm spot for 1 hour.

Remove the dough from the bowl. Sprinkle the raisins lightly with a tablespoon of flour. Knead the raisins and nuts into the dough.

Oil a large baking sheet or, preferably, a big round pizza pan. On a long counter, roll the dough back and forth under your palms into a cylinder that is 40 inches long. Taper one end slightly for the serpent's tail. Coil the dough into a circle on the baking sheet, and fatten the opposite end of the dough into a "head." This dough expands a good deal in baking, so leave the center hole as large as possible.

Brush the bread with egg yolk glaze. Press 3 or 4 dark raisins together into a ball, make another such ball, indent the dough on either side of the "head," and press in the raisins, making eyes for the serpent. Encircle the neck with a collar of raisins, and press in a raisin smile. Decorate the bread generously with candy confetti, colored sugar, or other decorations. Cover and let the bread rise for about 30 minutes.

Bake in a preheated 350°F oven for about 45 minutes. It may be necessary to cover the head and tail portions with foil if they threaten to overbrown.

Kulich

Makes 1 spectacular bread

This recipe makes one tall Kulich in a 2-pound coffee can. Kulich, a Russian Orthodox Easter bread, makes a good addition to a selection of holiday breads. Kulich and the Raisin and Spice Two-in-One Bread (page 107) are particularly handsome when displayed together.

4 cups unbleached flour
⅓ cup sugar
1 teaspoon salt
1 tablespoon lemon zest, grated
1 package plus 2 teaspoons yeast
⅔ cup milk
¼ cup water
3 tablespoons butter, cut into small bits
1 tablespoon Amaretto
1 egg, at room temperature
½ cup chopped blanched almonds

½ cup golden raisins
½ cup candied pineapple
¼ cup candied cherries, coarsely chopped

For the lemon glaze

1½ tablespoons lemon juice, strained
2 teaspoons water
3 drops vanilla extract
Generous ¾ cup confectioners' sugar

In a large bowl, combine 1 cup flour, sugar, salt, lemon zest, and yeast. In a saucepan, warm the milk, butter, and ¼ cup water until the butter has melted. Add the Amaretto to the liquid, then stir the liquid into the dry ingredients and beat vigorously with a heavy spoon. Add the egg and another ½ cup flour and continue to stir until the dough is smooth. Add the remaining flour and turn the dough out onto a work surface.

Knead for about 10 minutes, until the dough is smooth and elastic. (You will have to flour your hands frequently, but try not to add extra flour to the dough.) Put the dough in an oiled bowl, turn it over to grease its surface completely, cover, and let rise in a warm place for 1 hour.

Butter a 2-pound coffee can. Cut a doubled rim of aluminum foil and tie it around the top of the can so that it extends as a 3-inch collar above the rim.

Punch down the dough. Scatter nuts, raisins, pineapple, and cherries on a work surface and knead them into the dough. (The dough will feel rather damp; flour your hands as necessary.) Put the dough in the prepared can. Cover with plastic wrap and let the dough rise in a warm spot until it touches the plastic.

Bake in a preheated 350°F oven for 45 minutes. Let the bread cool in the can for 15 minutes, then unmold onto a rack. When cool, mix the lemon glaze ingredients and frost.

Raisin and Spice Two-in-One Bread

Makes 2 large loaves or 4 small loaves

For the base dough

2 packages yeast
⅓ cup warm water
1¼ cups half-and-half, warmed
About 9½ to 10 cups unbleached
  flour
2 eggs plus 2 egg yolks
1 cup milk
1¼ cups sugar
1 cup (2 sticks) unsalted butter,
  melted and cooled
2 teaspoons salt
1 teaspoon cinnamon
2 teaspoons lemon zest, grated
1 large apple, peeled, cored, and
  finely grated

For the raisin-nut loaf

1½ cups raisins (mixed light and
  dark)
1½ teaspoons cinnamon

3½ ounces almond paste
½ cup coarsely chopped toasted
  almonds

For the spice loaf

Pinch powdered saffron
¼ teaspoon ground cardamom
¼ teaspoon cinnamon
½ teaspoon ginger
2 good pinches ground cloves
Several gratings nutmeg
¼ teaspoon allspice
½ cup finely chopped black
  walnuts
1 generous cup sugar cubes
3 tablespoons Cognac

This practical recipe allows you to get a good deal of holiday baking done in one session. A large base dough is divided into two portions; half is flavored with spices and Cognac-doused sugar cubes; the other portion is laden with raisins and almonds. This recipe will yield 2 large spectacularly festive breads, or 4 loaf-pan-sized breads, which are perfect for holiday presents.

To make the base dough, put the yeast and warm water in a large mixing bowl. When the yeast dissolves, add the half-and-half and stir in 2 cups flour. Cover and let the sponge rise in a warm place for about 30 minutes, or until doubled in bulk.

Stir down the sponge and add the eggs and yolks, milk, sugar, butter, salt, cinnamon, and lemon zest. Squeeze the grated apple to rid it of excess moisture and add to mixture. Mix well, then stir in about 7 cups flour, or enough so that the dough is firm enough to turn out onto a floured board. Divide the dough into two portions, one slightly larger than the other.

Make raisin-nut bread using the smaller portion. Toss the raisins with cinnamon. Pinch the almond paste into small portions, then knead the almond paste, raisins, and almonds into the dough. Add flour as necessary to combat stickiness. Knead and work in flour for about 8 minutes, or until the palm of your hand pressed into the center of the dough comes out clean and the dough is smooth and elastic. Put the dough in a clean oiled bowl, cover with a towel, and set aside to rise for about 1½ hours.

Make spice bread from the remaining larger portion of base dough. Sprinkle all the spices over the dough. Add the walnuts to the work surface. Put the sugar cubes in a bowl and sprinkle all the Cognac over them. Knead the spices, walnuts, and sugar cubes into the dough, again adding in flour as necessary. Knead for about 8 minutes, or until smooth. Put the dough in an oiled bowl, cover, and set in a warm place to rise. This bread needs 1¼ hours to rise, so both breads will be ready to form at about the same time.

Shape the dough into four buttered 9 x 5 x 3-inch loaf pans, two for each bread. Or make two large loaves, one bread each in a buttered fluted brioche mold, savarin mold, or charlotte mold. Cover, and let loaves rise again for 50 minutes before baking.

Bake the loaves in a preheated 325°F oven. Large loaves will take 1¼ hours, small loaves around 50 minutes. Cover the raisin loaves with foil after 20 minutes so that the raisins do not overbrown.

You can, if you wish, drizzle these loaves with a simple confectioners' sugar frosting, flavored to taste with vanilla.

Simple White Frosting

| 2 cups confectioners' sugar | Water |
| 1 egg white | 1 teaspoon vanilla extract |

Stir together the confectioners' sugar and egg white, adding 3 to 4 tablespoons water gradually until a smooth frosting develops. Stir in vanilla extract. Drip the frosting over the loaves.

Pecan Sticky Buns

Makes 30 buns

1 package yeast
¼ cup warm water
3¾ cups all-purpose flour
1½ teaspoons salt
1 cup (2 sticks) butter, cut into
   small morsels
2 eggs, lightly beaten
½ cup sour cream
⅔ cup maple sugar or plain
   sugar

For the syrup
½ cup light brown sugar
1 cup maple syrup
2 tablespoons light corn syrup
4 tablespoons butter
¼ teaspoon cinnamon
2 cups well-chopped pecans

⅔ cup light brown sugar

This classic favorite delights children and adults alike.

Dissolve the yeast in warm water and set aside.

Mix the flour and salt in a bowl. Cut in the butter, working it into the flour with a pastry cutter or your fingertips until a uniform mixture results that looks like oatmeal. Make a well in the dry ingredients and blend in the eggs, sour cream, and yeast. Mix thoroughly and knead briefly until the dough seems very smooth. Wrap in plastic and chill the dough for at least 2 hours.

Lightly sprinkle a work surface with maple or plain sugar. Roll the dough out to a rectangle 12 or 13 inches long and 8 or 9 inches wide. Square up the corners as much as possible. Sprinkle the top of the dough with maple or plain sugar. Fold the dough envelope style so there are three layers. Turn the resulting dough long way up. Roll out again to a large rectangle, sprinkle with sugar, and fold up again, envelope style. Repeat this step one more time. Let the dough rest for 5 minutes.

Roll the dough out until it is uniformly ¼ inch thick. A rectangle approximately 15 inches long and 12 inches wide should result. Sprinkle on the remaining sugar and roll up the dough. Cut it into ½-inch slices to make 30 portions.

To prepare the syrup, combine brown sugar, maple syrup, corn syrup, and butter in a saucepan. Heat until the butter has melted and the syrup is hot and thin. Stir in the cinnamon.

Put about one tablespoon syrup in the bottom of each cup of a muffin tin. Add 1 tablespoon pecans to each cup. Put a dough portion in each cup. Top each dough portion with a good teaspoon of brown sugar. Cover and let the buns rise for 15 minutes. Preheat oven to 350°F.

Bake for 20 to 25 minutes. Serve warm.

Cinnamon Rolls or One Huge Sticky Bun

Makes 12 rolls or 1 huge bun

This recipe will make 1 dozen cinnamon rolls or 1 very large cinnamon sticky bun —you can easily double the recipe if you wish and make both. The grated apple disappears in the finished product, leaving moist, nondrying bread.

1 package yeast
¼ cup warm water
¾ cup milk
6 tablespoons unsalted butter
½ cup sugar
½ teaspoon salt
1 teaspoon cinnamon
1 egg, lightly beaten
1 small apple, peeled and finely grated
4 cups all-purpose flour
⅔ cup dark raisins

For the topping
4 tablespoons melted butter
1 teaspoon cinnamon, or to taste
1 cup sugar

For the glaze
1 egg yolk beaten with 2 teaspoons water

Dissolve the yeast in warm water in a large bowl or mixer bowl.

Put the milk, butter, and sugar in a saucepan and heat gently until the butter and sugar have melted. Let cool briefly, then add to the yeast. Add the salt, cinnamon, egg, and apple. Mix in half the flour and beat, either by hand or in an electric mixer, for 5 minutes. Add the remaining flour, turn the dough out onto a work surface, sprinkle on the raisins, and knead for 8 minutes, at which point the dough should be smooth, shiny, and elastic. Put the dough in an oiled bowl, turn the dough once so it is oiled on all sides, cover, and set in a warm place to rise for 1 hour. The dough should double in bulk.

Remove dough from the bowl and roll out to an 18-inch square.

To make cinnamon rolls, brush the dough with melted butter. Scatter on cinnamon and sugar and smooth evenly. Roll up the dough, then cut the roll into 12 slices, each 1½ inches wide. Arrange the rounds in a buttered 9 x 13-inch baking pan. Cover and let rise for 20 minutes. Brush the risen rolls with egg yolk glaze. Bake for 35 to 45 minutes in a preheated 350°F oven. Let cool, then frost with Hard White Icing.

Hard White Icing Bring 2 tablespoons water, 2 tablespoons butter, and a pinch of salt to boil. Remove from the heat and stir in 1 teaspoon lemon juice, 1½ teaspoons vanilla extract, and 1 generous cup sifted confectioners' sugar. Drizzle over and around the cinnamon rolls.

To make a giant sticky bun, roll out the dough to an 18-inch square. Brush on melted butter, then sprinkle evenly with cinnamon and sugar.

Cut the dough into nine strips, each 2 inches wide. Butter a 10-inch round springform pan. Roll up one strip and place it cut side up in the center of the pan. Curl the next strip around the first, and so on until all the strips form a continuous spiral.

Cover pan with a towel and leave to rise in a warm place for 20 to 30 minutes. The dough should reach the side of the pan and expand upward until even with the top of the pan. Bush with egg yolk glaze.

Bake in a preheated 350°F oven for around 45 minutes. Take the bun from the oven and immediately frost with Transparent Glaze.

Transparent Glaze Bring 2 tablespoons water, 1 tablespoon corn syrup, 1 tablespoon butter, and a pinch of salt to a boil. Remove from the heat and stir in 1 teaspoon lemon juice, 1½ teaspoons vanilla extract, and 1 cup sifted confectioners' sugar.

Praline Buns

Makes 12 buns

The dough for these big sticky, crunchy buns can be made ahead and baked later. These are excellent for a special breakfast.

1 package yeast
¼ cup warm water
2¼ cups all-purpose flour
3 tablespoons sugar
2 teaspoons baking powder
½ teaspoon salt
1 teaspoon cinnamon
⅓ cup unsalted butter, cut into small bits
⅓ cup warm milk
1 egg, lightly beaten

For the filling and topping
10 tablespoons (1¼ sticks) unsalted butter, softened
1⅓ cups packed brown sugar (preferably half light brown, half dark brown)

½ cup pecans, finely chopped
12 pecan halves

Dissolve the yeast in warm water. Sift together the flour, sugar, baking powder, salt, and cinnamon. Work in the butter with your fingertips until it is in very fine particles. Make a well in the center of the flour. Add the yeast, warm milk, and egg, and knead together until dough can be turned out onto a lightly floured work surface. Knead briefly (4 minutes), then put the dough in an oiled bowl, cover with a towel, and leave in a warm place to rise for 30 minutes.

To prepare the filling and topping, cream together the butter and brown sugar. Set aside ⅔ cup of the mixture, packed down.

Roll out the dough to a 10 x 15-inch rectangle. Spread the dough with the filling. Sprinkle on the chopped pecans, then neatly and tightly roll up the dough, the short way rather than the long way. Cut the roll into 12 slices, and place them on a buttered baking sheet with a rim. (At this point these could be covered with plastic wrap and refrigerated overnight.) Cover and let rise in a warm place for 45 minutes. (If the dough has been refrigerated, the rising time should be extended to 60 minutes.)

Preheat oven to 400°F. Sprinkle the top of each roll with a spoonful of the reserved sugar-butter mixture. Place a pecan half atop each bun. Bake for about 12 minutes, or until the buns are golden and the sugar has caramelized. Spoon any escaped caramel back over the buns. Serve warm.

Moravian Sugar Bread

Makes 1 large rectangle

This irresistibly delicious bread is full of cinnamon-sugar goodness. I first tasted it at the restored eighteenth-century Winklers Bakery in Winston-Salem, North Carolina, and it has been my favorite breakfast-brunch bread ever since.

1 package yeast
1 cup warm water
⅓ cup sugar
1 cup mashed potatoes (2 medium potatoes)
2 eggs, lightly beaten
Generous ½ teaspoon salt
8 tablespoons (1 stick) butter, softened
1 teaspoon vanilla extract

½ teaspoon cinnamon
3 cups all-purpose flour

For the topping
1 tablespoon milk
1⅓ cups packed light brown sugar
1 teaspoon cinnamon, or to taste
8 tablespoons (1 stick) melted butter

Dissolve the yeast in warm water, preferably in the bowl of an electric mixer. Add the sugar, mashed potatoes, eggs, salt, butter, vanilla, cinnamon, and 2 cups of flour. Stir vigorously with a heavy spoon until the dough is smooth, or beat for 5 minutes at medium speed. Scatter half the remaining flour over the dough, work it in somewhat, then turn the dough out onto a floured work surface and knead in the remaining flour. Work the dough well; it will be quite soft. Put it in a buttered bowl, cover, and let rise in a warm spot for a good hour.

You can make 1 or 2 breads from this amount of dough. I make 1 large (14 x 18-inch) rectangle, though you might also choose to make a large round shape.

Butter a baking sheet, jelly roll pan, pizza pan—or any pan with a small rim. Using your hands to ensure good rustic shaping, pat the dough and stretch it out until it is about ¾ inch thick.

For the topping, brush the dough with milk. In a bowl, combine the brown sugar and cinnamon, and mix well with your hands to fluff the sugar and remove any lumps. Scatter the sugar over the bread. Using a finger, make many indentations over the surface of the bread. Drizzle on the melted butter as evenly as possible. If you are a cinnamon lover (which I am), shake on a bit more cinnamon. Cover and let rise for 15 minutes.

Preheat the oven to 350°F.

Bake for 30 to 35 minutes, at which point the bread should be a mass of golden, half caramelized cinnamon slicks and the top of the bread should feel firm. Remove from the oven and spoon any escaped sugary mixture back up over the bread. Serve warm.

Cinnamon Sugar Sticks

Makes about 15 sticks

These sticks are crisp and half caramelized on the bottom, sugar-crunchy on top. Absolutely delicious, and they freeze well, too.

For the dough
1 package yeast
3 tablespoons sugar
¼ cup warm water
½ cup warm milk
½ teaspoon salt
¼ teaspoon cinnamon
5 tablespoons butter, softened

1 egg, slightly beaten
2¼ cups all-purpose flour

For the topping
4 ounces melted butter
1½ cups sugar mixed with 1
    tablespoon cinnamon

Stir yeast and sugar into the warm water and let sit for 10 minutes. Stir the yeast, then add warm milk, salt, cinnamon, 3 tablespoons softened butter, the egg, and 1 cup flour. Beat by hand or with a mixer for 5 minutes, then cover the bowl and set aside to rise in a warm place for 40 minutes.

Stir down, then add the remaining 1¼ cups flour and knead the dough for about 12 minutes on a lightly floured surface, until it is very elastic. Cover the dough with plastic wrap and chill in the refrigerator for 30 minutes.

Use the remaining 2 tablespoons softened butter to generously coat the bottom and sides of a 9 x 13-inch baking pan.

Lightly flour a work surface and roll out the dough to a 9 x 13-inch rectangle. Cut the dough across the 9-inch width into strips that are about ¾ inch wide, creating 15 strips.

To make the crisp topping, dip the dough lengths in melted butter. Sprinkle a work surface with part of the cinnamon sugar and press the strip into the mixture on both sides. Twist and twist the dough strip until it resembles a corkscrew, then lay the strip across the width of the pan. Continue until all the strips are in place. Scrape up any bits of cinnamon sugar that are left and scatter them over the surface. Cover, set in a warm place, and let rise until doubled in bulk, around 20 minutes, at which point the twists will have expanded into a solid bread.

Preheat the oven to 350°F. Bake the sticks for 25 minutes. Let rest in the pan for 5 minutes, then turn out. Serve slightly warm.

Sugar-Crusted Raisin Bread

Makes 1 loaf

Here is an old-fashioned rolled loaf of raisin bread that, when slit across its length just before baking, blossoms into a handsome sugar-crusted creation.

½ cup rum (dark or light)
½ cup hot water
1 cup raisins or currants
1 cup warm milk
2 tablespoons corn syrup
1 package yeast
Pinch nutmeg

3½ teaspoons cinnamon
1 egg, lightly beaten
About 3¼ cups unbleached flour
4 tablespoons melted unsalted
  butter
1 cup sugar

Put the rum and hot water in a bowl. Add the raisins and let them plump for 30 minutes. Drain well.

Put the warm milk and corn syrup in a bowl. Stir until the syrup dissolves. Add yeast and let it dissolve. Stir in the nutmeg, ½ teaspoon cinnamon, egg, drained raisins, and 3 cups flour. Mix well, then turn the dough out onto a work surface and knead for about 10 minutes, adding flour as necessary, until the dough is smooth and elastic. Put the dough in an oiled bowl, cover, and let rise in a warm place for about 1 hour, until doubled in bulk.

Remove dough from the bowl and roll it out on a clean surface to a rectangle 9 x 20 inches. Brush the dough with 1 tablespoon melted butter, leaving a ¾-inch-wide border free from butter all around the dough. Mix the sugar evenly with the remaining 3 teaspoons cinnamon. Spread two thirds of the cinnamon sugar over the buttered portion of the dough. Roll the dough up, starting from a short end. Transfer the 9-inch-long roll to a buttered 9 x 5 x 3-inch loaf pan, seam side up. Let dough rise in a warm spot for about 35 minutes, until it is nicely rounded up over the top of the pan.

Using a razor blade, slit the top of the loaf through the center length. Cut down through two or three layers of dough, then gently spread the layers apart with your hands. Cover, let the loaf rise for another 10 minutes, and slit through the center again, so that the entire slit is now about 1½ inches deep. Again spread the layers apart so they fan toward the sides. Cover and let the loaf rise for another 10 minutes. Just before putting the loaf to bake, scatter the remaining cinnamon sugar over the center slit and dribble on the remaining melted butter.

Bake the loaf in a preheated 350°F oven for 50 minutes.

The King's Cake

Makes 1 loaf

A chapter of festive breads would not be complete without a Gâteau de Roi, or King's Cake.

This "cake" (actually a yeasted sweet bread) is common on Twelfth Night, Epiphany, or, as some call it, Little Christmas. In Europe, Epiphany marks the celebration of the coming of the wise men bearing gifts to the Christ child twelve days after Christmas. In America, the King's Cake is offered most frequently in Louisiana, where it makes its appearance at Mardi Gras.

The commercial King's Cake available in Louisiana bakeries is a simple affair—a coffee cake baked in circular crown form and frosted with the rather garish stripes of Mardi Gras's purple, gold, and green. What is amusing about the ritual bread is that a miniature plastic baby is baked in its interior. Someone throws a party serving King's Cake, and whoever receives the slice in which the favor is hidden must then provide the next party, which also features a King's Cake—and so the celebration continues. (Rumor has it that a pecan used to be the favor in Louisiana King's Cakes, until too many stingy revelers simply swallowed the nut without owning up to their obligation to throw the next party.) Whether one celebrates Twelfth Night or not, the ritual bread, with its hidden favor designating good luck, wealth, or what you will, is a nice addition to festive family occasions.

1 batch of Cinnamon Sugar Sticks dough (page 113), with an additional ⅓ cup flour worked into the dough
Small plastic baby, or bean or coin

For the frosting
2 tablespoons unsalted butter

¼ cup boiling water
Sifted confectioners' sugar
½ teaspoon vanilla extract, or to taste
Yellow and green food coloring
Confetti or nonpareils colored sprinkles

Make a batch of Cinnamon Sugar Sticks dough, adding additional flour so that the dough is quite stiff. Let the dough rise once, then punch it down, hide the favor somewhere in its depths, and on an oiled baking sheet form the dough into the shape of a slightly oval ring. Cover, and let rise for about 40 minutes, until doubled in bulk, then bake bread in a preheated 350°F oven for 40 to 45 minutes. Let cool completely.

To make the frosting, stir the lump of butter into the boiling water and let it melt. Add enough confectioners' sugar to make a good glaze of spreading consistency. Beat the frosting well, preferably with an electric hand mixer, then add the vanilla.

Divide the frosting into 3 portions. Tint one yellow, one green, and leave the remaining portion white. (I find the traditional purple frosting garish, but you could, if you wish, mix a bit of blue and red coloring to see what results.) Frost the bread in 1½-inch-wide alternating stripes of yellow, green, and white. The frostings will blend together at the edges when they are spread on the bread. Sprinkle colored candies over the white portions.

Maple Bubble Bread Ring

Makes 1 large ring

A delicious, spectacular-looking bread that would be a handsome addition to an important breakfast or brunch or a wonderful present to give a friend.

1 package yeast
¼ cup warm water
1 cup milk
¼ cup sugar
½ teaspoon salt
⅓ cup (5½ tablespoons) unsalted butter
1 egg plus 1 egg yolk, lightly beaten

5 cups all-purpose flour

For the topping
4 tablespoons unsalted butter
⅔ cup dark brown sugar
¼ heaping teaspoon cinnamon
⅔ cup maple syrup

In a large bowl, dissolve the yeast in warm water. In a saucepan, scald the milk, turn off the heat, then add sugar, salt, and butter. Let cool somewhat and add to the yeast mixture. Stir in the egg and yolk and 2 cups flour, then beat vigorously. Add 2 more cups flour and mix until the dough leaves the sides of the bowl. Turn the dough out onto a floured work surface and continue to knead, sprinkling on flour, until the remaining cup is absorbed. Knead for 8 minutes. Put the dough in an oiled bowl and turn the dough over to oil the top. Cover with a towel and let rise for 1 hour. Butter a 12-cup (10-inch diameter) ring or savarin mold.

As the dough nears the end of its rising, prepare the topping. Melt 2 tablespoons butter in a small pan and set aside. Put the brown sugar and cinnamon in a wide bowl and mix with your fingertips until the sugar no longer clumps. Put the maple syrup and remaining 2 table-spoons butter in a pan, bring to a simmer, and cook at a soft rolling boil for 3 minutes.

Pinch off portions of dough approximately golf-ball size. Dip each ball in the melted butter, then roll in brown sugar until generously coated. Place the balls in the prepared mold until the bottom is covered with one layer. Pour half the maple syrup over the balls. Continue forming balls and build a second layer on top of the first. Stir any leftover brown sugar mixture into the remaining maple syrup and pour over the top of the balls. Let the bread rise until it reaches the top of the pan.

Preheat the oven to 350°F. Bake for 45 to 50 minutes. Let stand in the pan for 10 minutes, then place a rack over the mold and turn over mold and rack together. Release the bread over a bowl or other pan, as a bit of syrup may drip off the bread. Spoon any excess syrup back over the bread. Serve warm.

Cranberry, Almond, and Walnut Loaf

Makes 1 loaf

Juice of 1 large orange	2¼ cups unbleached flour
3 tablespoons melted unsalted butter	½ teaspoon salt
	½ teaspoon baking soda
1 teaspoon almond extract	1½ cups cranberries, washed and drained
1 cup sugar	
1 egg	½ cup walnuts, in large pieces

Preheat the oven to 325°F. Butter a 9 x 5 x 3-inch loaf pan.

Put the orange juice in a measuring cup. Add enough water to measure ¾ cup. Add the melted butter and almond extract and set aside.

In a bowl, mix together the sugar and egg until thick and lemon-colored. Stir in the orange juice.

Put the flour, salt, and baking soda in another mixing bowl. Add the cranberries and walnuts and gently mix them in the flour until they

This is a good holiday bread, one that is a bit more tart than some cranberry breads. It contains almond extract, which provides a sophisticated flavoring element.

are well coated. Make a well in the center of the dry ingredients and stir in the liquid ingredients. Stir briskly, just to the point that the ingredients are nicely mixed. Pour the batter into the prepared pan.

Bake for 1 hour and 10 minutes. Test the center of loaf by inserting a wooden skewer; if it comes out wet, bake for another 5 minutes.

Greek Honey Apricot Bread

Makes 1 bread

Apricot breads and pastries are common offerings in Greek coffee shops. This recipe yields a large, thin bread heavily coated with apricots that is delicious for breakfast or lunch.

1 package yeast
¼ cup warm water
2 tablespoons sugar
½ cup milk
2 tablespoons honey
3 tablespoons butter
½ teaspoon salt
½ teaspoon ginger
¾ teaspoon cinnamon
1 egg, lightly beaten
2¼ cups all-purpose flour

For the apricot coating
9 ounces dried apricots
½ cup honey
¼ teaspoon cinnamon
¾ cup sugar
⅓ cup blanched slivered almonds

For the glaze
1 egg yolk beaten with 2
   teaspoons water

Dissolve the yeast in warm water. Put the sugar, milk, honey, butter, and salt in a small pan and heat until the butter melts. Let cool slightly, then add to the yeast. Stir in the ginger, cinnamon, and egg. Stir in 1½ cups flour and beat vigorously by hand or with an electric mixer for 5 minutes. Cover the bowl and set aside to rise in a warm place for 40 minutes.

While the bread is rising, prepare the apricot coating. Put the dried apricots in a saucepan and just cover them with water. Cover the pan and simmer for about 40 minutes, until the apricots are perfectly tender and have absorbed the water. Stir frequently toward the end of the cooking period to make sure the fruit does not scorch. Add honey, cinnamon, and sugar to the apricots and cook for another 10 minutes. Stir in the slivered almonds.

Punch down the risen dough, add the remaining flour, and knead for about 10 minutes, until the dough is smooth and silky.

Oil a baking sheet or large round pizza pan. Using your hands, spread and flatten the dough out to a square 13 to 14 inches wide. Pat the dough into a 1-inch rim around the edge and pinch up divisions across the bread so the bread divides visually into quarters. Now gently stretch and round the outer rim of the bread until it resembles a four-leaf clover shape, with four large, slightly indented pockets.

Brush the dividing rim portions of the bread with egg yolk glaze. Divide the apricot mixture between the four indentations and spread the fruit out evenly to the borders.

Cover and let the bread rise in a warm place for 15 minutes. Preheat the oven to 350°F.

Bake for 30 minutes. This should be cooled slightly before serving so the apricot coating has a chance to firm somewhat.

Figgy Bread

Makes 1 loaf

12 ounces figs, stemmed and cut into small pieces ("white" figs —big yellow-brown ones—are preferable to black figs or figlets)

¾ cup sugar

8 tablespoons (1 stick) unsalted butter, softened

3 eggs

¼ teaspoon cinnamon

Several scrapings of nutmeg

1 teaspoon grated orange zest

1 tablespoon lemon juice

2 cups unbleached flour

1 teaspoon baking powder

¼ teaspoon baking soda

⅓ cup buttermilk

Put the figs, sugar, and ¾ cup water in a saucepan and cook over low heat for about 20 to 25 minutes, until the figs are soft. Purée the figs in a food processor or blender. Let cool briefly.

Butter a 9 x 5 x 3-inch loaf pan. Preheat the oven to 350°F. Using an electric mixer, cream the butter. Beat in one egg at a time. Mix in the fig purée, then add cinnamon, nutmeg, orange zest, and lemon juice.

Mix the flour and baking powder together. Stir the baking soda into the buttermilk.

Add half the flour mixture to the fig mixture and blend well. Stir in the buttermilk and then, moving rapidly, stir in the remaining flour just until everything is blended. Spoon the mixture into the prepared loaf pan. Smooth the top, and put in the oven to bake for 1 hour. Test bread's center with a wooden skewer. If batter clings to skewer, bake another 5 to 10 minutes.

This is a loaf that is moist and flavorful. It has a holiday "figgy pudding" spirit to it, but is much more rapidly prepared than a true steamed pudding. I like the combination of faint orange and fig and the way the tiny fig seeds lightly crunch in the mouth.

The Della Robbia Wreath

Makes 1 large wreath
(Color plate 22)

This beautiful wreath-shaped loaf will grace any holiday table. It is the most spectacular sweet bread presentation I know.

For the dough

1 package yeast
¼ cup warm water
½ cup warm milk
3 tablespoons sugar
½ teaspoon salt
½ teaspoon cinnamon
2 tablespoons melted unsalted butter
1 egg, slightly beaten
2⅓ cups unbleached flour

For the glaze

1 egg yolk beaten with 1 teaspoon water and ¼ teaspoon sugar

For the fruit

Choose from what is available to you among glacéed holiday fruits and nuts. Plump dried apricots and prunes in hot water. A good assortment might be:

2 slices pineapple
½ cup red glacéed cherries
¼ cup green glacéed cherries
4 glacéed orange slices
2 dried or glacéed pear halves
4 prunes, plumped
4 apricot halves, plumped
Dates
Dark and golden raisins, as needed
Walnut halves
Hazelnuts
Whole almonds
Gold or silver dragées

For the jelly glaze

½ cup red currant jelly
Red sugar crystals

In a large mixing bowl, dissolve the yeast in warm water. Stir the yeast, then add warm milk, sugar, salt, cinnamon, melted butter, and egg. Add 1 cup flour and beat well for 5 minutes. Cover the bowl, set it in a warm spot, and let rise for 40 minutes.

Stir down the batter, add the remaining 1⅓ cups flour, then turn the dough out and knead on a floured work surface for 10 minutes. Cover the dough with plastic wrap and chill in the refrigerator for 30 minutes.

On a lightly floured surface, roll out the dough to a 12-inch circle. Cut a 6½-inch circle out of the center and set aside for later use. Transfer the wreath-shaped dough to an oiled baking sheet. Brush the dough with egg yolk glaze.

Arrange fruits and nuts around the wreath as densely and artistically as possible. Thick pineapple slices should be sliced into thinner rounds. Cherries should be halved. Clusters of fruits are especially effective.

Cut leaf-shaped sections from the reserved dough and attach them to the wreath by moistening with egg yolk glaze and pressing them well into the dough. Place a few gold or silver dragées here and there for a gilding effect. Cover and let the bread rise for 20 minutes. Preheat the oven to 350°F.

Bake the bread for 25 to 30 minutes, at which point the visible bread portions should be a handsome golden brown. Remove from the oven, but leave on the baking sheet.

Heat the broiler.

Put ½ cup red currant jelly and 2 tablespoons of water in a small pan. Heat until melted. Brush the entire bread with jelly glaze. Put the bread under the broiler briefly to glaze and gild the fruit. Let the bread cool slightly, then sprinkle lightly with red sugar crystals. As the bread is heavy with fruit, it should cool and firm on the baking sheet before you remove it.

EXOTIC BREADS AND CRACKERS

There was an old Man of Calcutta,
Who perpetually ate bread and butter . . .
Edward Lear

For Chinese meals, Indian cur-
ries, and Middle Eastern feasts, it is particularly nice to prepare exotic
regional breads. Giant Golden Puffs and intricately twisted Coconut
Knots are marvelous accompaniments to curry; Onion Boards and Pita
Bread are splendid with Middle Eastern fare; and a stir-fried dish in
the Oriental manner would be nicely set off by Yin Yang Bread or a
steamer full of filled Chinese buns.

I particularly recommend the Armenian Cracker Bread, which is, I
believe, as good a rendering as any commercial cracker bread I have
sampled. Bake the bread and eat it crisp, or steam the bread and bend
its supple substance into tubes to be filled with feta cheese, tomatoes,
shredded lettuce, and Greek olives.

Curry Panettas

Makes 8 panettas

Panettas are panfried Indian breads. This version is a beautiful curry yellow. The more onions, the more curry, the more salt, the better I find these breads taste. Cut and sample a portion of your first fried panetta and adjust seasonings to suit your own taste. These are, of course, marvelous with curry, but they would also be good with a spiced fruit salad for lunch.

2 cups less 1 tablespoon all-purpose flour
½ teaspoon salt
4 tablespoons chilled unsalted butter, cut into bits
½ cup ice water

For the seasoned butter
8 tablespoons (1 stick) unsalted butter
⅓ cup peanut oil
2½ teaspoons curry powder
1 teaspoon lemon juice
½ teaspoon salt
⅓ cup very finely minced scallions

Mix the flour and salt in a bowl. Add the butter and, using your fingertips, work it into the dough, as you would for piecrust. When the butter has disappeared, sprinkle on the ice water and knead the dough into a ball. Continue kneading until dough is velvety smooth. Cover and set aside for 30 minutes.

To prepare seasoned butter, melt the butter in a saucepan. Add oil, curry powder, lemon juice, and salt and set aside.

Roll the dough into a cylinder and cut it in half. Roll each portion of dough back and forth under your fingertips until it is 1 inch in diameter. Cut each section of dough into 8 portions, for a total of 16 portions. Cover and let the dough rest for 5 minutes.

Roll out two portions to create two 5-inch circles. Brush the center of one circle with curry butter and add a small portion of minced scallions. Leave a ¾-inch border around the edge. Moisten the edge with a finger dipped in water, then place the other rolled round on top and press the edges together firmly. Continue rolling and forming breads until all are compiled.

Take the first bread and roll it out again, as thin as possible, to make a circle about 9 inches in diameter.

Heat 1 tablespoon curry butter in a 9-to-10-inch frying pan. Fry the rolled bread until it is golden on the bottom. Sprinkle the top with scallions and a bit of salt and turn the bread over, adding a bit more curry butter at this point, if necessary. Continue frying until browned and speckled on the other side, about 3 minutes frying time in all.

Continue rolling the other breads, wiping the pan as necessary, and frying each panetta until all are cooked. These can be served hot and fresh, or they can be made in the morning and reheated in a low oven for an evening supper.

Coconut Knots

Makes 6 or 7 knots
(Color plate 23)

1 package yeast
1 tablespoon sugar
1½ cups warm water
1 teaspoon salt
⅓ cup toasted shredded coconut

About 3¾ cups unbleached flour
1 cup (untoasted) shredded
  coconut
Peanut oil for frying

Dissolve the yeast and sugar in warm water in a large bowl. Add the salt and toasted coconut. Stir in 3 cups flour, or enough to make a dough that can be turned out onto a floured work surface. Knead for 10 minutes, adding flour, until a smooth, relatively firm dough results. Put the dough in an oiled bowl and let rise in a warm place for 1 hour, or until doubled in bulk.

On a lightly floured surface, roll the dough out into a rectangle roughly ½ inch thick. Cut strips of dough around ¾ inch wide and roll them under your palms to round them nicely. Attach 2 strips by moistening the ends with water and pressing them together. Curl the strips into interesting coiled shapes around 6 to 7 inches in diameter. Overlap into knotlike patterns, and at each point where the strips overlap, moisten and press together. Cover, and let breads rise for 30 minutes.

Bring a large pot of salted water to a bare simmer. Scatter the fresh coconut on a large plate. Gently place one of the bread knots in the water. Let it poach for 15 seconds, then remove it with a slotted spoon, immediately put it in the fresh coconut, then turn it over so that coconut adheres to both sides. (At this point the breads can be set aside for 3 to 4 hours before frying, if desired.) Continue until all breads are poached.

Heat a tablespoon of peanut oil in a frying pan and briefly fry one knot until it is brown and the coconut is toasted and golden on both sides. Continue, adding 1 tablespoon oil for each knot. Serve fresh.

These breads are not only delicious and exotic-looking, but also a great deal of fun to serve guests, for they allow people to "break bread together" by pulling apart portions from communal loaves. If I wanted to serve breads with a meal of Oriental character, these are the breads I would choose, but they also fit other exotic occasions and are good with fruit salad lunches.

Chinese Steamed Buns

Makes 16 buns
(Color plate 23)

These plump white buns are traditionally served in Chinese dim sum restaurants. Their soft, curious texture results from kneading in baking powder after the yeasted dough rises. You can fill them or not, as you choose. You will need a large Chinese steamer—or an improvisation—to carry out this operation. (A large roasting pan with a cover and fitted with a cake rack will suffice.)

1 envelope yeast
2 tablespoons sugar
1 cup warm water
1 tablespoon sesame oil
½ teaspoon salt
1 tablespoon soy sauce
4½ cups all-purpose flour

For the filling (optional)
3 ounces shiitake (forest) mushrooms

½ cup dried pork (available in Chinese produce stores)
1 teaspoon sugar
1½ teaspoons sesame oil
1 small garlic clove
2 scallions, minced
3 tablespoons soy sauce
1 teaspoon baking powder
Red and yellow food coloring

In a large bowl, dissolve the yeast and sugar in warm water. Stir, then add sesame oil, salt, soy sauce, and flour. Turn the dough out onto a floured board and knead for about 10 minutes. Put the dough in a greased bowl, cover with a damp tea towel, and let rise for 1 hour, or until doubled in size.

If a filling is desired, prepare it while the dough is rising. Cover the mushrooms with warm water and soak them for about 30 minutes, until soft. Reserve the soaking liquid. Cut off hard stems. Squeeze the mushrooms as dry as possible, then mince finely in a blender or food processor. Add the dried pork, sugar, oil, garlic, scallion, 1½ tablespoons reserved mushroom water, and soy sauce and blend to a paste.

Butter or oil twenty 4-inch squares of wax paper.

Punch down the dough. Sprinkle it with 1 teaspoon baking powder and knead for 10 minutes. Roll the dough out into a cylinder and cut into around 16 pieces. Cover dough portions with a towel and begin forming buns immediately.

If the buns are not to be filled, simply roll the portions into round balls. If they are to be filled, place one portion of dough on a lightly floured surface and roll into a circle 4 to 5 inches wide. Aim to leave the dough thin at the edges and thick in the middle. Place a portion of filling in the center, then lift and pleat the edges over the filling, pinching and twisting them together to secure the filling. Set each bun, pleat side down, on a square of wax paper. Place all the buns on wax paper, on steamer racks.

Cover the steamer and set in a warm place for the dough to rise for 45 minutes. If you wish to decorate the buns, mix a drop of red food coloring with a drop of yellow and dilute with 2 or 3 drops water. Using a paintbrush, paint a small motif on the top of each bun.

When the buns have risen, turn on the heat and let buns steam for 20 minutes. Carefully remove the steamer racks so as not to jar condensed water onto the buns. Let sit for 5 minutes before removing the cover. Serve the buns warm.

Giant Golden Puffs

Makes 6 large breads
(Color plate 23)

3 cups all-purpose flour	1½ teaspoons salt
2 eggs	½ cup warm water
2 tablespoons butter	About 2 quarts oil for frying,
3 tablespoons peanut oil	preferably peanut oil

Put the flour in a large bowl and make a well in the center. Add the eggs, butter, and 3 tablespoons oil. Mix with your hands until ingredients are well blended and small grainy particles form.

Dissolve the salt in warm water. Add to the flour mixture, sprinkling on a bit at a time, until a soft dough forms. Knead dough for 10 minutes, then divide into 6 portions.

Heat 2 quarts oil in a deep fryer or a large, heavy pan about 10 inches in diameter.

Roll out each dough portion into a rough oval shape. The dough should be rolled thin enough so that it is almost transparent. Moisten the rim of the dough with a finger dipped in water, then fold the dough over once and press edges together. Fold the dough over again, in the opposite direction. You should have a thin rough piece about 8 inches in uneven diameter. Repeat until all pieces are rolled and folded. Test the heat by dropping a piece of dough into the oil; it should bob to the surface with a soft easy spray of fine bubbles in motion around it. (Deep fryers should be around 375°F.) Gently place the rolled dough in the fat and fry until golden brown. Turn over and cook the other side. Do not let them fry to too dark a color. Lift out with a slotted spoon and drain on several layers of paper towel. Sprinkle lightly with salt. Continue frying the breads. If the breads are not to be eaten immediately, they can be reheated in the oven. Serve with any curried or exotic meal.

This version of Indian puri makes much larger breads than the small 5-to-6-inch rounds usually offered in Indian restaurants, though you could use the dough to make the classic smaller breads. The extra fold given these huge breads guarantees that they will puff spectacularly, and guests will enjoy breaking and sharing these at table.

Sesame Chuppaties

These large, free-form breads are quick to make and handsome included in an assortment of exotic breads. As they are perfect crackers, they also accompany cheeses nicely. The recipe can be varied by substituting rye flour for whole-wheat flour.

Makes 6 large chuppaties or more small ones
(Color plate 23)

¾ cup unbleached white flour
¾ cup whole-wheat flour
1½ teaspoons salt
1 tablespoon unsalted butter, cut
    into small pieces

2 teaspoons sesame oil
2 tablespoons tahini (See Note)
⅓ cup plus 2 tablespoons cold
    water

Mix the flours and salt in a bowl. Work in butter and oil with your fingertips until they completely disappear.

Dilute the tahini with water. Add to the dry ingredients and knead briefly to form a smooth, medium-soft dough. Wrap in plastic and set aside to rest for 1 hour.

Heat the broiler. Lightly oil a baking sheet. Divide the dough into 6 (or more) pieces. Roll out each section to a rough, vaguely circular shape. It should be rolled so thinly that the dough is almost transparent. Transfer the dough to the baking sheet and broil, 8 to 10 inches away from the flame. In less than a minute, the dough should be lightly browned at the edges and crisp. Turn the bread over and let it cook for about 1 minute on the other side.

Note: Tahini is a sesame paste available in health food or specialty food stores.

Scallion Pancakes

These classic Chinese pancakes, redolent of scallions and sesame oil, are delicious served as appetizers.

Makes 4 large pancakes, serves 6 to 8

2 cups all-purpose flour
⅔ cup cool water
1 tablespoon butter
2 tablespoons lard
1 tablespoon sesame oil

3 tablespoons minced scallions
    (white and tender green parts)
2 teaspoons salt
4 tablespoons peanut oil

Put the flour in a bowl. Make a well in the center and gradually stir in the water. Knead the dough until silken and elastic. Cover and let rest in a warm spot for 20 minutes.

Cream together the butter, lard, sesame oil, and scallions.

Divide the dough into 4 equal portions. (Keep portions not being rolled under plastic wrap.) Roll one portion into a thin 8-inch square. Sprinkle with ½ teaspoon salt, then press the salt into the dough with the heel of your hand. Spread the dough with one quarter of the scallion-lard mixture. Roll the square up, and pinch the ends of the roll together to seal them. Coil the roll into a circle, tuck the outer end under, and press to seal. Using a rolling pin, flatten the coil until it forms a thick pancake about ¼ inch thick and 7 to 8 inches wide. Cover the pancake with plastic wrap and roll and coil the remaining portions of dough.

Heat 1 tablespoon peanut oil in a skillet. Fry one pancake at a time. Turn the pancake over after 4 or 5 minutes so that each side turns golden brown. Repeat until all are fried. These may be held in a warming oven. Cut into wedges to serve.

Yin Yang Bread

Makes 1 loaf
(Color plate 23)

1 envelope yeast
1 cup warm water
1 teaspoon sugar
1½ tablespoons soy sauce
⅓ cup lightly packed dried pork

2 tablespoons sesame oil
3½ cups flour
1 egg, separated
About 2 tablespoons black
   sesame seeds

In a large bowl, dissolve the yeast in water. Add sugar, soy sauce, pork, and sesame oil. Work in the flour until dough is firm enough to turn out onto a work surface. Knead for around 8 minutes, or until smooth and elastic. Put the dough in an oiled bowl, cover, and let rise in a warm spot for 1 hour.

While the bread is rising, make the form for the yin yang pattern. Cut a 10-inch round of cardboard. With a pencil, dissect the circle into quarters. Draw curves on the cardboard so that the two sides are mirror images. Cut the cardboard into two pieces along the curved line. The two pieces should very nearly match.

When the dough has risen, place on an oiled baking sheet and roll and pat it out into a 10-inch circle. Lay one piece of the pattern on the dough to shield half the circle. Make an egg yolk glaze by beating the yolk with 2 teaspoons water. Brush the exposed side with the glaze, then cover the glaze with a solid coat of black sesame seeds. Lift off

The idea for this striking black and white bread was suggested to me by food writer and cookbook writer Barbara Tropp. Dried shredded pork is available at Oriental food stores.

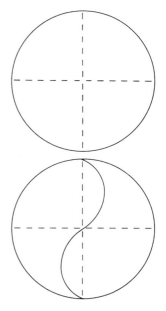

the cardboard shield and replace it gently so that it covers the black sesame seed area.

Beat the egg white with 2 teaspoons water. Brush the egg white glaze lightly over the clear side of the dough. Sift a solid layer of flour onto the exposed portion.

Let rise in a warm spot for 20 minutes. Preheat the oven to 350°F.

Bake for 40 to 45 minutes. Try not to jar the loaf when removing it from the oven, so that the black and white pattern remains pristine.

White Pizza

This savory "pizza bread" is delicious as an appetizer or as an accompaniment to a salad.

Serves 6

For the crust

2 teaspoons yeast
¼ teaspoon sugar
¾ cup warm water
1 tablespoon olive oil
1 teaspoon salt
About 3 cups all-purpose flour

For the topping

2 large onions, chopped
1 large garlic clove, chopped
½ cup olive oil
⅔ cup freshly grated Parmesan cheese
Black Niçoise olives (optional)

In a large bowl, dissolve the yeast and sugar in warm water. Add olive oil, salt, and enough flour to make a soft dough. Turn out onto a floured work surface and knead, working in flour, until a soft but unsticky dough results. Cover, set the dough in a warm place, and let rise for 45 minutes.

Cook onions and garlic in 3 tablespoons olive oil over very low heat. When cooked and limp, put the onions in a blender or food processor and purée. Set aside.

When the dough has risen, remove it from the bowl and pat and roll it into a rustic circle on a large pizza pan or baking sheet. Spread onion purée over the dough to within ¾ inch of the rim. Sprinkle Parmesan cheese over the onion. Drizzle with remaining olive oil. If you wish, scatter a handful of black Niçoise olives over the surface. Let rise while the oven heats.

Preheat the oven to 400°F. When the oven is hot, shove in the pizza and let it bake for 20 minutes, or until it is pale gold. Serve hot.

Onion Boards

Makes 4 onion boards
(Color plate 23)

1 package yeast
½ cup warm water
2 tablespoons sugar
½ cup milk
4 tablespoons unsalted butter
2 tablespoons grated onion
¼ teaspoon freshly ground
    pepper
3 teaspoons salt
2 eggs, separated
About 4¾ cups unbleached flour

For the topping
1½ sticks (¾ cup) unsalted
    butter
⅓ cup dried onion flakes
4 tablespoons coarse cornmeal
Poppy seeds
1 egg lightly beaten with 1
    tablespoon water

These soft, puffy flat breads are loaded with onions and poppy seeds. Absolutely delicious.

In a large bowl, dissolve the yeast in warm water. Put the sugar, milk, and butter in a saucepan and heat just until the butter has melted; stir in the grated onion. Add to the yeast, along with the pepper, salt, and egg yolks.

In another bowl, beat the egg whites until foamy. Add the whites to the liquid ingredients. Stir in flour until a dough forms that is thick enough to turn out on a work surface. Knead for 10 minutes, adding flour until the dough is elastic but still soft and pliable. Place in an oiled bowl, cover with a towel, and let rise in a warm place for 1 hour, or until doubled in bulk.

While the dough rises, start the topping preparation. Put the butter and onion flakes in a pan. Heat until the butter melts. Cook briefly to soften the   but do not let the butter brown. Remove from the heat and let onions soften in the butter.

Divide dough into 4 portions. Using your hands to achieve a more interesting texture, spread and gently stretch each portion out into a rough 9- to 10-inch shape that is vaguely round. Put 1 tablespoon cornmeal, a tablespoon of poppy seeds, and a tablespoon of the soft-ened onion on a work surface and mix with your fingers. Brush one side of a bread portion with egg and press the egg side down into the poppy seed mixture. Brush the other side with egg, then turn the bread over and press the other side in the mixture. Spread the seeds and onions as evenly as possible. Put the bread on an oiled baking sheet. Lightly sprinkle the top of the bread with salt; generously scatter on poppy seeds. Continue making the other breads. Let the breads rise for 20 minutes.

Preheat the oven to 375°F.

Just before putting breads in to bake, dribble the remaining onion butter over the tops of the breads. Bake for 15 to 18 minutes. The breads should be golden and puffy, the onions brown but not black.

Armenian Cracker Bread

Yields 4 large crackers
(Color plate 23)

I like Armenian Cracker Breads even better than pita breads. When baked, they form delicious sesame-flavored crackers that are splendid with cheese and keep a very long time. When steamed over hot water, they turn into soft flexible breads that can be rolled up and filled with all the trimmings of tacos or heros or pita pockets.

1 teaspoon yeast
1 tablespoon honey
½ cup warm water
1 tablespoon sesame oil
1 tablespoon melted unsalted
  butter
1 teaspoon salt

1¼ cups unbleached flour

For the glaze and topping
1 egg beaten with 1 tablespoon
  water

3 tablespoons sesame seeds

In a bowl, dissolve the yeast and honey in warm water. Stir well, then add sesame oil, melted butter, salt, and 1 cup flour. Mix into a dough, then turn it out onto a floured work surface and knead for 10 minutes, adding flour as necessary, until a smooth, medium-soft dough forms. Put the dough in an oiled bowl and turn the dough to oil all its surfaces. Cover bowl with a damp towel and let the dough rise in a warm place for 1 hour.

Lightly grease the back side of a large baking sheet. Place the dough on the sheet and roll out to a rectangle approximately 14 x 16 inches. The dough will be quite thin. Using your fingers, press gentle indentations all over the dough. Take a toothpick and prick holes about 2 inches apart over the surface. Cut the dough into 4 rectangular portions.

Brush dough with egg glaze, and scatter sesame seeds over the top. Let the dough rise for 20 minutes.

Preheat the oven to 375°F. Bake for 12 to 15 minutes, or until golden brown. Check the crackers during baking to assure that one portion does not overbrown due to uneven heating. Cool and store in an airtight container.

To Soften Crackers Bring a steamer or large pot with 2 inches of water in it to a boil. Lay a rack across the top, if using a pot. Place 1 or more breads in the steamer. Cover, then allow to steam for 5 to 10 minutes, or until breads are flexible enough to roll easily. Stuff with desired filling and roll up.

Plate 22. *The Della Robbia Wreath. A spectacular, sweet holiday bread.*

Plate 23. *Exotic Breads and Crackers. (top shelf, from left) Sesame Chuppaties; Chinese Steamed Buns; Armenian Cracker Bread; Pasta Machine Crackers. (middle shelf, from left) Coconut Knots; Spiral Breads; Giant Golden Puffs; a Yin Yang Bread. (bottom shelf, from left) Onion Boards; more Coconut Knots.*

Plate 24. *Cretan Bread Wreath.*
Plate 25. *"Trencher" Bread Mats.*
Plate 26. *A Miniature Bakery.*

Pita Bread

Makes 10 pita breads

1½ packages yeast
1 teaspoon sugar
2 cups warm water
2½ teaspoons salt

2 tablespoons peanut oil
4½ cups unbleached flour
Cornmeal

This recipe makes large, fully puffed pitas that are excellent for stuffing.

In a large bowl, dissolve the yeast and sugar in warm water. Add salt and oil, then stir in enough flour so that the dough can be turned out onto a work surface. Knead for 10 minutes, adding flour, until a pliable dough of medium-firm consistency results. Divide the dough into 10 portions and shape each into a flattened ball.

Using a heavy rolling pin and exerting firm pressure, roll out each portion to a rough circle approximately 7 to 8 inches in diameter. Sprinkle baking sheets lightly with cornmeal and place each pita on the baking sheet as it is finished. Cover the rolled portions lightly with a kitchen towel.

Let the breads rise for 30 minutes. Preheat the oven to 475°F. Have two racks in the oven, one of which should be at the lowest level.

Place one tray of breads on the lowest rack. Bake for 5 minutes. Raise the tray to upper rack and, at the same time, place a new tray of breads on the lower rack. Bake for another 5 minutes. Remove the top tray of finished breads, then raise the lower tray to continue baking at the upper level.

Immediately place finished pitas on a counter and cover them at once with damp kitchen towels. Let the breads steam under the towels until their crusts have softened and the breads are completely cool. Store in plastic bags in the refrigerator.

Yogurt Crackers

Makes 1 dozen crackers

1 teaspoon yeast
1 teaspoon sugar
2 tablespoons warm water
⅓ cup yogurt
¼ cup vegetable oil
½ cup gluten flour
1 tablespoon powdered malt
1 teaspoon salt

⅓ cup couscous (uncooked)
1 cup whole-wheat flour

For the glaze

1 egg yolk beaten with 2
    teaspoons water
Caraway seeds
Salt

These are rough, rustic, grainy cracker-biscuits. They would be excellent in a basket filled with assorted breads set out to accompany cheeses.

In a mixing bowl, dissolve the yeast and sugar in warm water. Stir in the yogurt and vegetable oil. Add the gluten flour, malt, salt, and couscous, then knead in the whole-wheat flour. Turn out onto a work surface and knead the dough for 8 minutes. Sprinkle a bit of flour on the surface as necessary, but try to keep additional flour to a minimum.

Roll the dough out to a rectangle approximately 12 x 15 inches. Transfer the dough to a lightly oiled baking sheet, square up the edges and sides as much as possible, then score the dough in half down its length. Space 5 scoring cuts perpendicular to the long cut so that the dough is divided into 12 crackers, each 6 inches long by approximately 2½ inches wide. (Scoring cuts will make it easier to break portions evenly later.)

Brush the top of the crackers with egg yolk glaze, and sprinkle lightly with caraway seeds and a bit of salt. Cover and let the crackers rise for 20 minutes.

Bake in a 350°F oven for around 15 minutes. Turn the crackers over and bake for 10 more minutes, until golden brown.

Pasta Machine Crackers

Makes 12 to 15 crackers
(Color plate 23)

This recipe was devised to prove that pasta machines have more than one use. If you wish, you can cut a center circle from each cracker before you bake them, then string up the crackers on a rope or tasseled silken cord to make a handsome presentation.

½ cup hot water
¼ teaspoon baking soda
1 tablespoon powdered malt
1½ teaspoons yeast
4 tablespoons melted butter
1 teaspoon salt

½ teaspoon sugar
About 1⅔ cups flour

For the glaze
1 egg yolk beaten with 2 tablespoons milk

Put the hot water in a mixing bowl. Add baking soda and stir until dissolved. Add malt. When the water cools to lukewarm, add the yeast and let dissolve. Stir in melted butter, salt, and sugar. Add flour and knead until the dough is smooth and elastic, soft but not sticky. Set the dough in a lightly greased bowl, cover with a towel, and let rise in a warm place for 45 minutes.

Divide dough in half. Set up a pasta machine with the kneading blade at its widest opening. Run half the dough through the kneading blade three times. Fold the strip in half and run through the next three successive openings. Lay the strip out on a counter and repeat kneading process with other half of the dough.

Dough strips may be cut into squares or large rounds. Place cut crackers on a baking tray. Prick the crackers with a fork in a decorative pattern. Brush with egg yolk glaze. Cover and let rise in a warm place for 20 minutes.

Preheat the oven to 350°F. Bake for 5 minutes, then turn the crackers over and bake for another 5 minutes. Let cool, then immediately store in an airtight container if crackers are not to be eaten at once. These are best fresh, or at least rewarmed to crisp them before eating.

Spiral Breads

Makes 4 or 5 spirals
(Color plate 23)

4 cups flour
1 tablespoon baking powder
1 teaspoon salt
½ cup milk

1½ cups water
2 tablespoons vegetable oil or melted lard

Heat the broiler or grill.

Mix the flour, baking powder, and salt in a bowl. Make a well in the center. Add the milk, water, and oil and mix well and rapidly until the ingredients are perfectly blended. Give the dough 10 light kneading strokes. Roll out the dough to a rectangle approximately 14 inches long and 7 to 8 inches wide. Cut lengthwise into 4 or 5 long 1½- to 2-inch strips.

Breads may be spiraled around a stick, broom handle, or rolling pin. Cover baking object with foil so exposed portions of stick will not singe. Wrap and press a strip of dough around the stick, leaving space between each coil. Hold the stick near the heat source. As each side turns golden brown, turn the stick until all portions are toasted. Slip spiral bread off the end of the stick. Continue forming and toasting breads.

These breads are especially delicious dipped in garlic butter. They may be brushed with the butter, then held in a warming oven until all are cooked.

These spiraling breads, made famous around campfires, can also be cooked under the broiler or over a charcoal grill. As they are basically composed of biscuit dough, a small child might be allowed to make a spiral bread with a portion of dough from a regular biscuit batch.

SAVORY BREAD DISHES

Stolen waters are sweet, and bread eaten in secret is pleasant.
Proverbs

I love the wonderful economy of the dishes in this chapter—dishes from a variety of cultures that frugally turn leftover bread into sauces and pâtés, savory tarts and delectable desserts. I would particularly recommend for brunches the Bread and Cheese "Soufflé," which can be flavored and expanded with leftovers in a multitude of ways. I also enjoy serving *Gratin au Pain* to unsuspecting guests—it looks like mashed potatoes, is textured like mashed potatoes, and tastes amazingly good alongside roast meats of various kinds.

Two hollowed festive loaves—one filled with sour cream and green vegetables, the other with corned beef and mustard—are always appreciated at parties.

If you have never made a frying pan crumb crust, I suggest trying the Tartared Shrimp Tart or the Apple Tart, both of which are one-dish creations in which a bread crumb base has been solidified with either egg or caramelized sugar, respectively.

Sour Cream–Green Vegetable Dip in a Bread Case

Serves 12 to 15 as an hors d'oeuvre

This is my favorite mixture for dipping bread into. The water chestnuts are a particularly good and crunchy textural addition. I tend to make a double recipe of this for most parties, because it disappears so fast.

For the dip

10 ounces fresh spinach
1 cup mayonnaise
1 cup sour cream
8 ounces diced water chestnuts (if canned, drain and dry chestnuts)
2 tablespoons minced onion
1 tablespoon minced parsley
1 large garlic clove, peeled

¼ teaspoon paprika
1 teaspoon salt
½ teaspoon celery salt
Freshly ground pepper

1 round loaf white or sourdough bread
2 sticks (1 cup) unsalted butter

Stem and wash the spinach. Put the spinach in a large pot and cook it, using only the water that clings to the leaves. When just tender and still bright green, transfer the spinach to a colander and run a stream of cold water over the greens to set their color. Take up spinach by handfuls and squeeze it as dry as possible. Mince.

Combine mayonnaise, sour cream, spinach, water chestnuts, onion, and parsley. Put the garlic clove in a press and squeeze in half the garlic. Add paprika, salt, celery salt, and several grindings of pepper. Refrigerate the dip for at least 30 minutes. Taste for seasoning before serving.

To prepare the bread case, cut a lid from the top of the round bread, then hollow out the interior by pulling out portions of crumb that are large—two- or three-bite-sized pieces, as uniform in size as possible. Melt the butter in a pan and squeeze in garlic remaining in the garlic press. Brush the inside of the bread case with the garlic butter, and dip the pulled bread sections into the butter. Set case and bread portions on a baking sheet and bake in a preheated 350°F oven just until the pulled bread portions are tinged a light gold. Let cool briefly.

Fill the bread case with the green vegetable dip and serve. After the pulled bread portions are used, the bread case should also be broken off in portions and used to scoop out the filling.

Corned Beef and Mustard Dip in a Rye Bread Case

For the filling

1½ cups sour cream
1¼ cups mayonnaise
2 tablespoons minced onion
2 tablespoons minced parsley
1½ tablespoons Dijon-style mustard
5 ounces corned beef, shredded
3 ounces dried beef, shredded
1 teaspoon red wine vinegar
4 ounces diced Swiss or Gruyère cheese

2 teaspoons Worcestershire sauce
¼ teaspoon Tabasco sauce
Salt and freshly ground pepper to taste

1 round loaf light or medium rye bread
2 sticks (1 cup) melted unsalted butter

Here is another excellent mixture to use as a bread dip. It has a hearty beef and mustard flavor and is especially good served in a light or medium rye case.

Combine all filling ingredients. Mix well, cover, and refrigerate for at least 30 minutes. Taste carefully for seasoning, and add mustard, Tabasco sauce, or other seasonings as desired.

To prepare the bread case, cut a lid from the round of bread, then pull out large portions (2- to 3-bite-sized pieces) of the crumb until the loaf is just a shell. Brush the interior with melted butter, then dip the crumb portions in butter. Place all bread on a baking sheet and bake in a preheated 350°F oven until the crumb portions are crisp. Remove from the oven and let cool briefly.

Fill the bread with the dip mixture and serve.

OTHER BREAD "UTENSILS"

When bread is used as a case, as it was in the previous two recipes, it functions as a utensil. Here are three more functional uses to which you may want to put bread.

The Bread Snail Holder

Cut ½-inch-thick slices from a round loaf and fit them into individual buttered gratin dishes. Carve out indentations in the bread and spread slices with snail butter (butter seasoned with garlic, parsley, and shallots). Place snails and snail butter in each. Bake until the snails are hot and the bread is golden brown.

The Breaded Onion Soup Collar

If you have round soup bowls with handles, this is a pretty presentation you can create. Cut ½-inch-thick slices from a firm white loaf. Cut out circles from the center of the slices so that a slice can fit as a collar around the outside of the top rim of the soup bowl. Brush the top of the bread "collar" with melted butter and sprinkle with Parmesan cheese. Fill the bowls with onion soup and top with a slice of bread sprinkled with cheese. Toast in the oven or under a broiler until the collar turns into a crisp browned crust that is delicious broken off and dipped into the soup.

The Chili Bread Bowl

Buy or make small round loaves of white bread that can serve as individual containers for chili. Cut lids from loaves and hollow out each one. Line breads with thin slices of cheddar cheese. Place breads in a preheated 350°F oven and let the cheese melt into the bread. Fill the loaves with hot chili. Place a dollop of sour cream on top of the chili, and set the bread lid ajar on top of the chili bread bowl. Serve.

Crusty Cornbread Dressing Balls

Here is a tasty way to use up leftover cornbread. These balls are delicious served with a Southern-style fried chicken or fish dinner, and not nearly so prosaic as hush puppies.

Makes 16 balls

1 stick unsalted butter plus 2 tablespoons	1 teaspoon rubbed sage
1½ cups chopped celery	1 teaspoon salt
1 cup chopped onions	Freshly ground pepper
¼ cup chopped parsley	3 cups finely crumbled cornbread
	1 egg, lightly beaten

Heat 1 stick butter in a large skillet. Add the celery and onions and cook over low heat until tender.

Preheat the oven to 350°F.

Take vegetables off the heat and add parsley, sage, salt, a generous grind of pepper, cornbread, and the egg. Mix until well blended. Form mixture into 16 balls and arrange on a greased baking sheet. Place a small piece of the remaining cold butter on top of each ball. Cover the balls lightly with aluminum foil and bake for 30 minutes. Remove foil and bake for another 15 minutes so the balls can brown. Serve hot.

Alsatian Onion Bread

Makes 6 first-course servings

1½ cups coarsely chopped onions	⅔ cup unbleached flour
3½ tablespoons butter	1 teaspoon baking powder
2 tablespoons lard	¼ cup milk
1 teaspoon salt	¾ cup sour cream
Freshly ground pepper	1 egg

Put the onions, 2 tablespoons butter, and lard in a frying pan and cook the onions over medium-low heat until soft and of a golden transparency. Season with ⅓ teaspoon salt and several grinds of fresh pepper. Spread the onions on a 9-inch gratin or pie dish.

In a mixing bowl, combine the flour, baking powder, and another ⅓ teaspoon salt. Cut in the remaining 1½ tablespoons butter and work until it is well blended and almost disappears into the dry ingredients. Make a well in the center, add the milk, and stir to make a soft dough.

Knead the dough on a floured work surface for half a minute, then roll the dough out into a thin circle the correct size to completely cover the pie dish. Place the biscuit dough over the onion mixture. Prick holes all over the dough with a skewer.

Beat the sour cream and egg together. Stir in the remaining ⅓ teaspoon salt and several grinds of pepper, then pour the mixture over the top of the biscuit dough.

Bake for 15 minutes, or until speckled with brown on the surface. Cut into wedges and serve.

This is a delectable compilation of golden fried onions covered with a thin biscuit crust and then topped with sour cream and eggs. It bakes into a tasty dish that could be cut into small wedges and served as an hors d'oeuvre or first course, or it could accompany red meat, rather like Yorkshire pudding. This recipe is adapted from chef Louis P. De Gouy's The Gold Cook Book. He calls it Alsatian Onion Bread, but my suspicion is that its geographic origins are more nearly American Southern.

Bread and Cheese "Soufflé"

Serves 5 to 6

This is a comforting, delicious alternative to macaroni and cheese, but is more sophisticated in flavor. It can be made with slightly stale bread, fresh, homemade bread, or commercial whole-wheat or white bread. You can, if you wish, make small variations in the seasoning—a bit of paprika or curry instead of mustard; Tabasco or Worcestershire sauce to taste; perhaps a dice of hard sausage. Note that this dish can be made the night before or the morning of.

6 to 8 slices home-style bread, trimmed of crust	1 cup milk
4 tablespoons unsalted butter, soft and spreadable	⅔ cup heavy cream
	1 tablespoon grated onion
2 cups grated sharp cheddar cheese, or a mix of cheddar and Gruyère	3 teaspoons Dijon mustard, or to taste
	1 teaspoon salt
Freshly ground pepper	2 to 3 scrapings nutmeg
4 eggs	Pinch of cayenne pepper

Butter a 2-quart soufflé or casserole dish.

Spread the bread slices with butter. Place half the bread in the bottom of the soufflé dish. Scatter on half the cheese and grind on some pepper. Top with the remaining bread and the rest of the cheese.

In a bowl, combine the eggs, milk, cream, onion, mustard, salt, nutmeg, and cayenne pepper. Beat with a whisk or electric mixer until well blended and frothy. Pour the eggs over the cheese and gently press down on the cheese so that all of it is moistened. Cover and let stand for at least 1 hour before baking. It is even better to allow it to rest for 2 hours, and overnight is fine.

Preheat the oven to 350°F. Bake for around 50 minutes, or until a knife blade inserted in the center comes out clean.

Rye Bread Pancakes

Makes 4 to 6 servings

Put some leftover rye bread crumbs to soak overnight, add the other ingredients the next morning, and you will have delicious, economical pancakes with a hearty peasant taste. Whole-wheat crumbs can be substituted for rye crumbs if you wish.

1 cup light rye bread crumbs	1 teaspoon baking soda
½ cup buttermilk	1 teaspoon sugar
½ cup milk	¼ teaspoon salt
1 egg	½ cup all-purpose flour
1½ tablespoons melted butter	Butter or oil for frying

The night before you make the pancakes, put the rye bread crumbs, buttermilk, and whole milk in a bowl. Stir to combine, then cover the bowl and let the crumbs sit overnight.

The next morning, using a heavy spoon or pestle, press the crumb mixture through a sieve so the mixture will be uniformly grained. Stir the egg and melted butter into the crumb mixture.

In a mixing bowl, stir together the baking soda, sugar, salt, and flour. Make a well in the center, then add the liquid ingredients to the flour mixture, stirring just until blended.

Heat butter or oil in a frying pan and fry pancakes of medium size until light brown on both sides. Serve hot with butter and syrup.

Gratin au Pain

Serves 6 to 8

1½ pounds bread, homemade white or firm commercial
2¼ cups milk
2 tablespoons unsalted butter
10 ounces grated Gruyère cheese
1 teaspoon salt

Nutmeg
Freshly ground pepper
3 eggs, lightly beaten
⅓ cup heavy cream
¾ cup dry white wine

Remove the crust from the bread, cut the bread into ½-inch cubes, and put them in a large bowl. Bring the milk to a boil and pour over the bread. Cover the bowl with a plate or lid, and let it sit for 15 minutes.

Preheat the oven to 375°F.

Stir in the butter, two thirds of the cheese, salt, several scrapings of nutmeg, and a goodly amount of pepper. Mix eggs, cream, and wine and stir into the bread until the whole batter is well mixed.

Generously butter a 10-inch quiche or gratin dish and pour in the bread. Scatter the remaining cheese over the top.

Bake for 30 minutes, or until the top is nicely gilded a deep golden brown.

This is a delicious way to use up an overabundance of bread, or bread that is somewhat dry. You can serve this dish in place of potatoes with a red meat, or as a luncheon or late supper dish with an accompanying green salad and white wine. Guests will be mystified by the contents, for the dish is amazingly like mashed potatoes.

Scalloped Bread and Onions

Serves 8 to 10

3½ to 4 pounds onions
2 sticks (1 cup) unsalted butter
⅓ cup sugar
1½ teaspoons salt

Freshly ground pepper
1 large (28 ounces) can tomatoes
4 cups firm bread crumbs

Peel the onions and slice them thinly. Put the onions and 1½ sticks butter in a heavy pot and stir over low heat until the butter has melted. Cover the pot and continue simmering, stirring occasionally, for around

This is a good comforting dish that children as well as adults enjoy. It makes delicious use of drying bread, and is good reheated.

15 minutes, until the onions are very limp. Uncover the pot and add sugar. Continue cooking for another 15 minutes, stirring frequently, until the onions turn to a pale straw gold color.

Preheat the oven to 350°F.

Add salt and pepper to onions. Pour off ½ cup tomato juice from canned tomatoes and discard or use for other purposes; add the remaining contents of the can to the onions and break up the tomatoes into small portions. Stir in 2½ cups bread crumbs. Pour the mixture into a large gratin or quiche dish and smooth the surface. Sprinkle on the remaining 1½ cups bread crumbs. Melt the remaining ½ stick butter and drizzle over the crumbs.

Bake for 40 to 45 minutes, or until the crust turns golden brown.

Bread Pâté

A *delicious and economically meaty dish that can be served hot as a main course or cold and sliced as a pâté or in sandwiches with mustard and cornichons.*

Serves 8 to 10

3 eggs	½ teaspoon poppy seeds
½ cup milk	1 teaspoon sesame seeds
½ cup strong beef or chicken stock	Generous ¼ teaspoon celery seeds
1 tablespoon Cognac (optional)	1 tablespoon finely grated onion
2 cups firm white bread crumbs	1 tablespoon minced parsley
2 cups pecans	Freshly ground pepper
1 teaspoon salt	⅓ cup melted unsalted butter

In a large bowl, beat together the eggs and milk. Stir in the stock and Cognac. Add the bread crumbs and set aside to soak for 10 minutes.

Preheat the oven to 350°F.

In a blender or food processor, grind the pecans until they resemble a coarse grain like steel-cut oats or bulgur wheat. Stir the pecans, salt, poppy seeds, sesame seeds, celery seeds, onion, parsley, and several good grinds of pepper into the bread crumbs.

Grease a loaf pan with 2 tablespoons melted butter. Pour in the bread batter. Spoon another tablespoon of melted butter over the top.

Bake for 40 minutes, and twice during the baking time baste with the remaining butter. Tip the pan so the butter disappears down the sides of the pâté, and poke a few holes with a toothpick over the top to let the butter soak in. Use all the butter.

If the pâté is not to be eaten immediately, let it cool briefly, then turn out of pan. Wrap, refrigerate, and slice as needed.

Tartared Shrimp Tart in a Bread Crust

Serves 4 to 6

6 tablespoons unsalted butter
2½ cups medium-coarse white
    bread crumbs (around 5 slices
    firm home-style bread)
2 tablespoons olive oil
¾ pound peeled, deveined
    shrimp
1 egg plus 1 egg white
1 cup heavy cream

2 tablespoons tartar sauce
½ teaspoon salt
1½ teaspoons minced scallions
2 tablespoons finely minced
    parsley
Freshly ground pepper
1 slice bread
1 lemon, sliced

Melt the butter in a 10-inch frying pan. Add the bread crumbs and
stir them to coat evenly with butter. Cook, continuously stirring, over
medium heat until the crumbs are all lightly toasted. Remove the pan
from heat and, using the back of a spoon, press the crumbs evenly
over the bottom of the frying pan and up the sides about ½ inch. Set
aside.

In another frying pan, heat the olive oil and sauté the shrimp briefly
over high heat until they turn deep pink. Arrange the cooked shrimp
attractively on top of the crumb crust.

In a bowl, whisk together the egg, egg white, cream, tartar sauce,
salt, scallions, and parsley. Pour the mixture over the shrimp. Cover
the frying pan and set it to cook on a very low burner. Cook the tart
for 30 minutes, at which point the crumbs around the edge of the pan
will have browned, and the eggy center of the tart will be firm. (Be
careful not to drip condensed water from the lid onto the surface of the
tart.)

Just before the tart has finished cooking, grind fresh pepper over the
top and crumble the slice of bread evenly over the surface. Place the
pan briefly under the hot broiler (protect the pan's handle with foil, if
necessary). In less than 2 minutes the top crumbs will absorb the excess
butter, then brown into a handsome, speckled surface.

Let the tart rest briefly to solidify, then give the pan a gentle shake;
the tart should move freely in the pan. Place a platter on top of the
frying pan, then turn the pan and platter over together to release the
tart. Place a serving dish over the reversed tart and turn the two dishes
over together so the tart is right side up. Serve hot or lukewarm, with
lemon slices and additional tartar sauce, if you wish.

*Bread crumb tart
bases are a delicious
alternative to pastry
bases for tarts and
quiches. Here is a
version using shrimp
as a filling, but you
might also try cheese,
crab, or spinach
interiors. This is an
excellent luncheon
dish.*

In her 1925 book, *The Gentle Art of Cookery, the English writer Mrs. Leyel had a rather odd remark to make about bread sauce: "This is one of the sauces we make better in England than in France, for the French don't have bread sauce at all. . . ." Peculiar though this logic may be, bread sauce is a delicious and economical concept —all one needs as the starchy accompaniment to a golden roasted chicken, especially in hot weather.*

English Bread Sauce

Makes about 2½ cups

1 medium onion, coarsely
   chopped
3 cloves
2 cups milk
1 scrape nutmeg
Pinch freshly ground black
   pepper
Pinch cayenne pepper
¼ teaspoon salt

Pinch sage
4 slices firm white bread, dried in
   a slow oven, then finely
   pulverized in a food processor
2 tablespoons unsalted butter, cut
   into pieces
About 2 tablespoons heavy cream
Salt and pepper

Put the onion, cloves, and milk in a saucepan and bring to a boil. Reduce the heat and simmer for 5 minutes. Add the nutmeg, black pepper, cayenne pepper, salt, and sage and cook over very low heat for another 5 minutes. Stir frequently.

Strain the milk into a clean saucepan. Bring milk to a boil, remove from the heat, then add the dried bread crumbs all at once. Stir vigorously. Add the butter, and when it has melted into the sauce, add the cream, plus salt and pepper to taste. Bread sauce should be quite thick, but not so thick that it cannot move sluggishly when it is ladled. Serve hot or cold.

A good and rapidly executed dessert using fresh or half-dry bread. The juices of the apples combine with the bread to make a caramelized crust and a gentle, homey dessert.

Frying Pan Apple Tart in a Crumb Crust

Serves 4 to 5

6 tablespoons unsalted butter
2½ cups medium-coarse bread
   crumbs (around 5 slices firm,
   homemade-style bread)
½ cup plus 1 tablespoon sugar

2 cups grated peeled apples
   (preferably Winesap)
¾ teaspoon cinnamon
Pinch salt

Melt the butter in a 9-inch nonstick frying pan. Add the crumbs and let them toast until golden brown. Using a fork, pack the crumbs evenly over the bottom and up the sides of the pan to the height of 1 inch. Sprinkle the crust with 1 tablespoon sugar and set aside until needed.

Put the grated apples, remaining ½ cup sugar, cinnamon, and salt in a saucepan and cook for about 10 minutes over medium-low heat, or until the apples are thick, with no watery juices evident in the pan. Spoon the apples into the crumb crust and smooth the surface. With a fork press down any crumbs extending above the apple filling so the rim is even with the apples.

Place frying pan over low heat and let the bottom crust toast. Give the pan a small shake from time to time. The tart should feel like a solid unit, and the crust around the edge should brown faintly after 25 to 30 minutes.

Invert a platter over the frying pan. Carefully turn the platter and frying pan over together; the tart should slip neatly into the center of its serving dish. Serve warm, with a pitcher of heavy cream on the side.

Puffed French Toast

Serves 3 to 4

6 eggs, separated and at room
   temperature
1 tablespoon sugar
1 cup milk
½ teaspoon salt
1½ teaspoon vanilla extract

¼ teaspoon very finely grated
   orange zest
6 thick (1-inch) slices French
   bread
Butter

Prepare this toast the evening before and let it absorb the flavored eggs all night. In the morning, fry the rich, thick slices in butter.

In a mixing bowl, beat the egg whites until foamy and doubled in volume. Add sugar and continue beating until soft peaks form.

In another bowl, beat the egg yolks with milk, salt, vanilla, and orange zest. Fold the whites into the yolks.

Pour half the eggs into a 9 x 13-inch baking pan. Place bread slices in a single layer in the pan. Pour the remaining eggs evenly over the top. Cover lightly with plastic wrap and refrigerate overnight.

Fry the bread in butter over slow heat (about 4 minutes a side) until completely golden. Serve with unsalted butter and the syrup of your choice.

Most people will eat 2 slices.

Bread and Jam Omelet

Serves 6

¼ pound dried or drying bread (4 to 5 slices)
½ cup milk
½ teaspoon vanilla extract
1 teaspoon grated lemon zest
2 tablespoons sugar
2 eggs, separated

3 tablespoons butter
About 2 tablespoons confectioners' sugar
Jam of choice (orange marmalade or raspberry preserves are particularly good)

This is a homey, comforting Dutch dessert that utilizes dried bread. As it is composed of basic staples, it can make a handy last-minute dessert.

Crumble the bread into a bowl. Bring the milk to a boil in a saucepan, then pour it over the bread. Mash the bread and milk together with a fork until the mass is well blended and resembles cooked oatmeal. Stir in the vanilla, lemon zest, and sugar. Mix in the egg yolks.

Beat the egg whites until stiff. Stir half of them into the bread, then rapidly fold in the remaining whites.

Preheat the broiler.

Heat 3 tablespoons butter in a 10-inch frying or omelet pan. Pour in the bread-egg mixture and let it cook over low heat until the sides are firmly set and the omelet has only a thin top layer of uncooked egg. Because this is a thick mixture, the cooking time should not be hurried. Move the pan frequently on the heat so the bottom center does not scorch. Slide the omelet under the broiler briefly (around 30 seconds) to set the top.

Serve the omelet directly from the pan, or, making sure the omelet is loose, reverse it out onto a serving dish. Sift confectioners' sugar over the top. Cut into slices and top each slice with a spoon of jam. Serve either hot or cold.

Raspberry Bread

Serves 6 to 8

2 packages (10 ounces each) frozen red raspberries
8 slices firm white bread (homemade or commercial, cut slightly thicker than sandwich slices)

5 to 6 tablespoons unsalted butter
4 tablespoons sugar
1 teaspoon cinnamon
⅔ cup heavy cream

This easy dessert is similar to English Summer Pudding but shorter both in preparation and in macerating time.

Thaw the raspberries. Press them through a sieve to remove all seeds.

Trim the bread slices of their crusts. Melt 2 tablespoons butter in a frying pan and sauté the bread slices in batches. Allow each slice to absorb a good quantity of butter evenly on both sides. Add butter as needed and fry until all slices are a medium gold color.

Coat half the bread slices with raspberry purée. Arrange the slices, purée side down, in a ceramic or glass gratin or baking dish. Coat the top side of the slices with purée.

In a small bowl, combine the sugar and cinnamon. Reserve 1 tablespoon and sprinkle half of the rest over the raspberry bread.

Coat one side of the remaining bread with purée. Place it, purée down, in the gratin. Pour all the remaining purée over the top of the bread. Sprinkle on the other half of the cinnamon sugar. Cover the dish with plastic wrap and refrigerate. In 30 minutes, spoon up any raspberry liquid at the edges of the dish and sprinkle it over the top of the bread. Re-cover, and refrigerate for at least 2 hours more, or overnight if you wish.

Just before serving, whip the cream, sweeten with the reserved 1 tablespoon cinnamon sugar, and spread whipped cream over the top.

Superlative Bread Pudding

Makes 6 servings

Bread pudding needn't be a timorous mousy thing. Glorify the old English nursery dish with spices and Grand Marnier and you will have a dessert fit for the grandest adult company.

1⅓ cups milk
Zest of ½ lemon, grated
¼ teaspoon cinnamon
Pinch ground ginger
3 tablespoons sugar
Pinch salt
2 teaspoons Grand Marnier
1 teaspoon vanilla extract
½ cup heavy cream
4 eggs

6 slices white bread (good commercial bread or homemade bread), cut thinly
3 tablespoons unsalted butter, very soft
2 tablespoons raisins
Freshly grated nutmeg
½ cup heavy cream, whipped (optional)

Put the milk, lemon zest, cinnamon, ginger, sugar, and salt in a saucepan. Heat to scalding, then remove from the heat and let sit for 5 minutes. Add the Grand Marnier, vanilla extract, cream, and eggs, stirring constantly to keep the eggs from scrambling.

Cut the crusts from the bread slices. Butter them generously on one side, and cut each slice in two diagonally. Butter a 10- or 11-inch gratin dish. Arrange the bread, buttered side up, in the dish. Scatter raisins over the top.

Holding a sieve over the bread, strain the milk and egg mixture through the sieve and over the bread, making sure it covers and soaks the bread as evenly as possible. Pass 2 or 3 scrapings of nutmeg over the surface. Let sit at least 1 hour (preferably 2) before baking. (This pudding can also be refrigerated overnight before baking.)

Preheat the oven to 375°F. Bake for 30 minutes. Serve warm. Add a dollop of whipped cream on top of each serving, if you wish.

Steamed Whole-Wheat Bread Pudding with Raisin Sauce

I greatly admire the ingenuity of the following dish, which is adapted from the 1911 Cook Book of Left-overs. Herewith a loaf that might otherwise go to waste is dramatically rescued, stuffed full of raisins, soaked in spiced eggs and cream, and triumphantly steamed into a firm, sliceable pudding. I would not hesitate to set this dish before company.

Serves 8 to 10

⅔ to ¾ loaf of unsliced whole-wheat bread, preferably somewhat dried
⅓ cup dark raisins
2 eggs
4 tablespoons sugar
½ teaspoon salt
¾ teaspoon cinnamon
¼ teaspoon ginger
2 to 3 scrapings nutmeg
2 cups milk

For the raisin sauce
⅓ cup dark raisins
⅓ cup light brown sugar
2 teaspoons all-purpose flour
Pinch salt
Pinch cinnamon
2 tablespoons butter

Whipped cream

Cut off all the crust from the whole-wheat loaf. With a finger, gently poke holes an inch or so deep over the entire surface of the bread, and insert 2 or 3 raisins in each hole.

In a deep bowl, stir together the eggs, sugar, salt, and spices. Whisk in the milk. Place raisin-studded loaf in the egg mixture and let it soak for about 30 minutes, or until the entire amount is absorbed. Turn the loaf as necessary, and spoon egg up over the top frequently.

Transfer the soft, soaked loaf to a well-buttered 1½- to 2-quart charlotte mold or soufflé dish. Cover the dish with a layer of wax paper or aluminum foil, and tie the paper around the edge with a string to secure it.

Place the mold in a large pan that has a cover. Pour water around the mold until it reaches halfway up the sides of the mold. Place the large pan over gentle heat, cover, and let the bread steam for 1 hour.

If the mold rattles in the pan, or if the water simmers around the mold, turn down the heat.

While the pudding cooks, prepare the raisin sauce. Put the raisins and 1½ cups water in a saucepan and let them simmer over low heat for 15 minutes. Add the sugar and simmer for another 15 minutes. Dissolve the flour in 1 tablespoon water. Stir the flour into the raisins, add salt and cinnamon, and stir until smooth. Add the butter and stir until it melts and thickens the sauce.

When the pudding has finished steaming, unmold it onto a rimmed platter. Spoon the raisin sauce over the top. The raisins will remain neatly on the surface to provide a dense decoration; the caramelized sauce will drip down the sides of the warm pudding and form a moat around its edge. Serve warm, with stiffly whipped cream.

DECORATIVE BREADS

For those who like to play with and manipulate dough, nothing is more pleasing than to create a sculpted bread so handsome that it warrants keeping as an art object. It is, of course, possible to create artistic breads from regular bread dough and then paint them with an acrylic coating for preservation, but the objects tend to wind up looking like plastic imitations of themselves.

The Bread Sculptor's Clay (page 154) that seems to me most practical for forming various objects is based on rather tacky ingredients and principles, but it bakes hard, does not attract insects, and is most realistically breadlike as it colors in the oven. I use it to make large objects such as "trenchers," small objects like miniature breads, and highly decorated objects like Grecian wreathes.

The Bread Sculptor's Dough (page 154) is a purer medium and also works well for making nonedible bread sculptures, though it must be carefully preserved from ravaging bugs.

Bread Sculptor's Clay

16 slices store-bought bread, of the cheapest variety, preferably day-old

8 ounces white glue
Flour

Cut the crusts from the bread. If the bread is moist and fresh, spread the slices out to dry for a period of time. Turn them over once so both sides can firm somewhat. Crumb the bread in a food processor. Remove the crumbs and place them either in the bowl of a mixer or in just a large mixing bowl.

Add the entire contents of the glue bottle (cut across the top of the bottle and run a finger around the inside so every drop of glue is used). If you have an electric mixer, attach the kneading blade and mix briefly until the dough forms a stiff ball. If mixing by hand, literally use your hand to knead and manipulate the ingredients into a cohesive ball. (Hand kneading will take a while.)

When the bread starts to stiffen into a claylike substance, sprinkle some flour on a work surface and place the dough on it. Continue to knead in flour as necessary until the dough is stiff and unsticky. Wrap the dough in plastic wrap, place it in a plastic bag, and store in the refrigerator. This clay will keep 6 months and will make a good batch of miniature breads or one decorated "trencher" place mat.

Bread Sculptor's Dough

3 cups all-purpose flour
1 cup salt

About 1 cup plus 3 tablespoons water

Mix flour and salt in a bowl. Make a well in the center and add water until a stiff but kneadable dough results. Knead for about 8 minutes, until smooth and firm. Place the dough in a plastic bag, squeeze out air from the bag, then seal and place in the refrigerator at least overnight, to allow the salt to dissolve into the dough.

Objects made from dough can be baked immediately in a very low (300°F) oven until hard and pale gold. To make miniature breads, use all techniques and shapes of real bread.

The dough will keep 2 or 3 months refrigerated in an airtight container.

A Miniature Bakery

(Color plate 26)

The miniature bakery is one of several hidden delights in my kitchen. It sits on a low but open shelf, almost obscured from view. Visiting children, particularly little girls, love to discover it, and they will spend endless time arranging and rearranging the tiny breads to suit their own aesthetic sense. The breads are easy to make from Bread Sculptor's Dough or Bread Sculptor's Clay.

The bakery itself is made from an old discarded wooden box about 15 inches long. I invested $18 in miniature dollhouse furniture—armoires, bakers' racks, baskets, and tables—for the store's fixtures. This concept makes an imaginative gift for a child; you might include a small pot of Bread Sculptor's Dough so that he or she can make more bread to sell when the current stock has disappeared.

To Make Miniature Breads

Employ all the techniques and shapes used to make real loaves. Miniature breads may be brushed with egg yolk glaze, rolled in rye flour before baking, pressed in poppy seeds; or finished in any other way that intrigues you. The shapes are best made by rolling small portions under the palm or cutting and shaping them with a knife tip.

Bake small breads at a very low temperature (250° to 300°F) until hard and pale gold. Watch your batch of breads carefully; smaller breads will bake faster than larger ones. The breads will tend to brown better on the bottom, so turn the larger ones over halfway through baking to control color. Inch-wide breads can bake for 40 to 50 minutes. Small pea-sized rolls may need only 15 minutes.

Trencher Bread Mats

(Color plate 25)

In the Middle Ages, trenchers of bread were frequently used as containers for food at table. Each person had his own bread "bowl," a large thick round of bread with the top crust sliced off. Savory dishes would be served atop the trencher, and their juices would soak into the crumb. Each day the tasty saturated crumbs would be scraped out and eaten at the end of the meal; then the trencher would be stored for use at the next meal. At the end of the week, what remained of the trencher would be broken into morsels for the dogs, and a new trencher would be provided for the following week.

While true trenchers are hardly practical in this age (unless one intends to hold a medieval feast), the idea of place mats made of bread remains intriguing. They are particularly handsome at rustic meals of soups or stews. When made with Bread Sculptor's Clay, they are next to indestructible.

Each large trencher mat with a decorative edging requires one recipe of Bread Sculptor's Clay (page 154).

To make a mat, roll out the dough on a floured surface to ¼-inch thickness. Transfer dough to a large baking sheet and cut a round circle 14 to 15 inches in diameter. Gently prick the surface of the mat with the tip of a knife. Use the scraps to decorate the rim of the mat if you like. I like to roll long strands of "stems" and "leaves" and attach them around the edge at random, then shape heads of wheat, snip them into kernels, and attach them to the stems.

To attach decorations to the mat, rough up both surfaces slightly by gently scraping a knife across the two portions of dough where they will meet. Dampen a finger with water and lightly press the two doughs together.

The bread mats will be most handsome if they are brushed with an egg yolk and water glaze. Bake each mat at 300°F for at least 50 to 60 minutes to ensure its dryness. Watch the mat as it bakes, for if portions tend to bubble up, you must prick them with a knife to allow the air underneath to escape and ensure as much flatness as possible. Raised decorative portions may tend to start overbrowning, so have a supply of aluminum foil handy and tear off portions to cover and protect any spots that threaten to burn.

Remove the mats from the oven and let cool. These should store indefinitely if sufficiently baked. It is best to bake trenchers on a dry day.

Cretan Bread Wreath

(Color plate 24)

Some of the handsomest bread wreaths I know are made on the isle of Crete. Embossed on a circle of dough are doves and lilies, leaves and bows; and a gift of the pretty Cretan bread means anything from "Thank You" to "Happy New Home" to "Long Life." It is probably necessary to have a certain amount of artistic ability to form a professional-looking wreath, but you can also create a handsome wreath when you allow it to have a certain naïve folk art quality about it.

Roll out one recipe Bread Sculptor's Clay (page 154) to ¼ inch thickness. Transfer the dough to a baking sheet. Cut a circle 8 to 10 inches in diameter. Cut another circle out of the center to create a doughnut form. The "doughnut" can be 1½ to 2 inches wide, depending on the size of the original circle.

With the extra dough, form a variety of small doves with outstretched wings, seashell-like objects, bows, hearts, heads of wheat, and leaves. Arrange these around the doughnut until the pattern is pleasing, then start attaching the objects one by one.

Scratch the surface of the doughnut with the tip of a knife until it is slightly rough. Scratch the bottom of each object to be attached. Using your finger, lightly moisten the two surfaces with water, then gently press the surfaces together. When all the objects are attached, fill in any empty spots with small leaves or balls of dough. Indent the centers of the balls with a skewer so that there is a design over the entire surface. Lightly apply a glaze of egg white beaten with a tablespoon of water and brush over the surface.

Bake in a 250°F oven for an hour. If you wish, halfway through the baking, brush the raised portions of the design lightly with egg yolk beaten with 1 teaspoon water, to throw the design into relief. If any parts of the design start to overbrown, tuck small pieces of aluminum foil over the surface. Keep a frequent watch on the wreath as it bakes so it will color uniformly. This wreath should keep indefinitely.

INDEX